Criminalizing Motherhood and Reproduction

In this book, motherhood and reproduction are identified as sites of legal, political, and ideological surveillance, regulation, and criminalization. Collectively, this rich and diverse edited volume builds on cross-disciplinary frameworks and an attention to differences among mothers to analyze multiple ways that mothers and pregnant women face culture, policy, or practices that may criminalize their identities or their actions.

Several themes cross the volumes' six chapters, from the importance of problems related to socialized expectations of what "good mothers" should do – for incarcerated, formerly incarcerated, and never incarcerated mothers alike – to the role of state actors and everyday informal interactions in enforcing these expectations, particularly against marginalized, Black, Brown and young mothers in open-air prisons. Conflicts between motherhood ideologies and state control dominate many women under carceral motherhood. Nation-states are also implicated in these analyses, particularly in the European Union, where nation-states outsource abortion across and within geopolitical borders, making migration a contested strategy for pregnant women. Yet despite the criminalization of motherhood and reproduction described in the text, women and mothers are also found to be resilient, choosing their identities and their actions.

Criminalizing Motherhood and Reproduction will be a key resource for researchers, scholars, and practitioners in the fields of feminist criminology and motherhood studies, criminology and criminal justice, women's studies, gender studies, child and youth studies, and sociology. It was originally published as a special issue of *Women & Criminal Justice.*

Michelle Hughes Miller is Professor of Women's, Gender, and Sexuality Studies at the University of South Florida, USA. As a feminist criminologist, she analyzes cultural and systemic responses to "bad" mothers and responses to violence against women. Along with multiple publications, she co-edited *Bad Mothers: Representations, Regulations and Resistance* (2017).

Criminalizing Motherhood and Reproduction

Edited by
Michelle Hughes Miller

Routledge
Taylor & Francis Group
LONDON AND NEW YORK

First published 2024
by Routledge
4 Park Square, Milton Park, Abingdon, Oxon, OX14 4RN

and by Routledge
605 Third Avenue, New York, NY 10158

Routledge is an imprint of the Taylor & Francis Group, an informa business

British Library Cataloguing in Publication Data
A catalogue record for this book is available from the British Library

ISBN13: 978-1-032-69673-7 (hbk)
ISBN13: 978-1-032-69674-4 (pbk)
ISBN13: 978-1-032-69675-1 (ebk)

DOI: 10.4324/9781032696751

Typeset in Minion Pro
by codeMantra

Publisher's Note
The publisher accepts responsibility for any inconsistencies that may have arisen during the conversion of this book from journal articles to book chapters, namely the inclusion of journal terminology.

Disclaimer
Every effort has been made to contact copyright holders for their permission to reprint material in this book. The publishers would be grateful to hear from any copyright holder who is not here acknowledged and will undertake to rectify any errors or omissions in future editions of this book.

Contents

Citation Information

The chapters in this book were originally published in the journal *Women & Criminal Justice*, volume 30, issue 5 (2020). When citing this material, please use the original page numbering for each article, as follows:

Introduction

Introduction to Special Issue: Criminalizing Motherhood and Reproduction
Michelle Hughes Miller
Women & Criminal Justice, volume 30, issue 5 (2020) pp. 310–315

Chapter 1

Intensive Parenting Ideologies and Risks for Recidivism among Justice-Involved Mothers
Elizabeth A. Adams
Women & Criminal Justice, volume 30, issue 5 (2020) pp. 316–335

Chapter 2

Managing Motherhood: How Incarcerated Mothers Negotiate Maternal Role-Identities with Their Children's Caregivers
Ebonie Cunningham Stringer
Women & Criminal Justice, volume 30, issue 5 (2020) pp. 336–355

Chapter 3

Creating and Undoing Legacies of Resilience: Black Women as Martyrs in the Black Community Under Oppressive Social Control
Leah Iman Aniefuna, M. Amari Aniefuna, and Jason M. Williams
Women & Criminal Justice, volume 30, issue 5 (2020) pp. 356–373

Chapter 4

Discourses of Good Motherhood and the Policing of Young Parenthood
Amber-Lee Varadi, Rebecca Raby, and Christine Tardif-Williams
Women & Criminal Justice, volume 30, issue 5 (2020) pp. 374–390

Chapter 5

Criminalization of Women Accessing Abortion and Enforced Mobility within the European Union and the United Kingdom
Lula Mecinska, Carolyne James, and Kate Mukungu
Women & Criminal Justice, volume 30, issue 5 (2020) pp. 391–406

Notes on Contributors

Elizabeth A. Adams, Department of Criminal Justice, Temple University, Philadelphia, USA.

Leah Iman Aniefuna, Teachers College, Columbia University, USA.

M. Amari Aniefuna, Teachers College, Columbia University, USA.

Carolyne James, Institute of Business, Industry and Leadership, University of Cumbria, Carlisle, UK.

Lula Mecinska, Institute of Business, Industry and Leadership, University of Cumbria, Carlisle, UK.

Michelle Hughes Miller, Department of Women's, Gender, & Sexuality Studies, University of South Florida, Tampa, USA.

Kate Mukungu, Riverside Community Health Project, UK.

Rebecca Raby, Faculty of Social Sciences, Brock University, St. Catharines, Canada.

Ebonie Cunningham Stringer, College of the Liberal Arts, Penn State Berks, Reading, USA.

Amber-Lee Varadi, Department of Sociology, York University, Toronto, Canada.

Christine Tardif-Williams, Faculty of Social Sciences, Brock University, St. Catharines, Canada.

Jason M. Williams, Justice Studies Department, Montclair State University, USA.

Introduction to Criminalizing Motherhood and Reproduction

Michelle Hughes Miller

This special issue of *Women & Criminal Justice* is dedicated to analyzing the legal and extra-legal policies and practices that regulate mothers and pregnant individuals, and the effects of those regulations on women's lived experiences. A surveillance culture that dictates good and bad mothering linked—however directly—to regulatory or enforcement mechanisms may criminalize the identities, actions, and decisions of mothers—what Lerner refers to as a "war on moms" (2010). Thus, it is imperative that as feminist criminologists we consider what happens when we criminalize motherhood and reproductive choice, including for women who are already under state-control. Recognizing how these criminalizing activities collaborate with existing systems of oppression is key to identifying strategies for change.

One of my goals for this special issue was to publish research that broadens the intersection between two important substantive areas: feminist criminology and motherhood studies. Readers of this journal will be very familiar with feminist criminology (see e.g. Burgess-Proctor 2010; Potter 2015; Renzetti 2018), and have certainly been exposed in the last few decades to some excellent scholarship on motherhood and reproduction. Case in point was Clarice Feinman's edited volume, *The Criminalization of a Woman's Body* (that began as two issues in *Women & Criminal Justice* in 1992) which brought together several authors to discuss various pregnancy-related regulatory concerns, from drug use to abortion to surrogacy. More recently we have the thought-provoking 2017 *Women & Criminal Justice* "Policing Women's Bodies" special issue, edited by Meda Chesney-Lind (2017). These volumes emphasized issues of criminalized reproduction more explicitly, an approach that Mecinska, James and Mukungu (2020) also take.

However, readers may be less familiar with how motherhood studies has dealt with the topics addressed in this special issue. A lack of exposure to motherhood studies research is not surprising, as Kawash (2011, p. 970) found that motherhood as a topic of feminist research "had drifted to the margins of feminist studies" in general during the first decade of the new century. A more recent analysis shows this dearth of published research on motherhood has continued in feminist journals, with an average of 3.9% of articles published on motherhood from 2006 to 2016 across five leading feminist journals (O'Reilly, 2016, p. 194). And my own experience of presenting papers on motherhood at the annual meetings of the American Society of Criminology eventually led to me organize my own sessions—because there were few available that were dedicated to furthering research on criminalized/ing motherhood, or that recognized motherhood itself as a site of criminalization.

But within motherhood studies, contemporary scholarship builds on a long history of motherhood scholars who have considered how mothers, mothering and motherhood are defined and regulated by actors both within and outside the criminal legal system. Grounding this motherhood scholarship is a comprehensive critique of the institution of motherhood itself guided by the foundational work of Adrienne Rich (1976) in *Of Woman Born*, who first posited that the institution of patriarchal motherhood affected the lived experiences of mothers in largely detrimental ways. Other early motherhood scholars, like Pat Hill Collins (1990), Sara Ruddick (1995), Phyllis Chesler (1991), Sharon Hays (1996), and Barbara Katz Rothman (1989), separately discussed how mothers are "policed" ideologically also, leading to a more inclusive and intersectional conversation about how the governance of motherhood and reproduction is managed (see e.g. Bromwich, 2020). Today, motherhood studies includes vibrant theoretical and empirical scholarship that considers how "bad" mothers are produced, which mothers are more likely to be criminalized, and why such criminalization occurs (see e.g. Hughes Miller et al., 2017).

It is, of course, incorrect to say that scholars have not worked across these disciplinary divides before. Indeed, state-control of mothers or pregnant individuals is the clear epicenter of the Venn diagram between feminist criminology and motherhood studies, and an area of research that has resulted in rich empirical data, theoretically diverse explanations, and astute and humane policy-driven recommendations. Indeed, the last 20 years have resulted in outstanding scholarship on "carceral motherhood" (Brown & Bloom, 2009), such as Sandra Enos' (2001), *Mothering from the Inside*. Recent books demonstrate significant growth in this fruitful substantive area, including Venezia Michalsen's astute *Mothering and Desistance in Reentry* (Routledge, 2019) and various edited volumes published by Demeter Press, the first feminist press dedicated to scholarship on motherhood and reproduction. A prime example of Demeter Press relevant volumes is Joanne Minaker and Bryan Hogeveen's far-ranging *Criminalized Mothers, Criminalizing Mothering* (2015). Two of the articles in this special issue (Adams, Cunningham Stringer) further this important, cross-disciplinary look at how identities, practices, and beliefs of justice-involved mothers are affected by their interactions with the criminal legal system.

Even more powerful, however, is the way scholars across areas of expertise have frequently embraced intersectionality as a theoretical and/or methodological framework for their work. I think of *Killing the Black Body* by Dorothy Roberts (1997) as a foundational intersectional text in this substantive area because of her intensely researched and poignant arguments about how Black motherhood and Black reproduction have been intentionally criminalized. More recently, Andrea Ritchie in *Invisible No More* (2017) has taken on the policing of Black motherhood, describing in detail the relationship between police brutality and the denigration of mothers of color. Other scholars have highlighted that oppressed mothers, including mothers who may be indigenous, working-class, queer, or disabled, have been labeled "unfit" mothers, and faced with the possibility of losing their children through the actions of criminal legal system, medical, or child welfare authorities (see e.g. Bromwich, 2017; Hughes Miller 2020). Aniefuna, Aniefuna, and Williams (2020) build on such research to consider contemporary criminalizing experiences of Black women and mothers in one urban community.

Despite these points of overlap, however, more integrative, cross-disciplinary scholarship is needed, especially scholarship that considers both state-sponsored and extra-institutional criminalization, and work that centers the lived experiences of mothers who are already oppressed. For instance, it is important that scholars look beyond institutional actors for evidence of regulation and control, such as Wong's (2012, p. 95) work on reimagining Foucault's panopticon as "the ubiquitous 'observational gaze' that mothers are constricted into by virtue of gender and fertility."

Here, Varadi, Raby and Tardif-Williams consider how young mothers experience this type of panopticon and the corresponding policing of societal expectations and demands. All of this research must more consistently use intersectional approaches so we can further unpack the differences among mothers in their experiences of and responses to various forms of social control. That said, I hope the articles in this special issue take us a bit further down this path, and I would like to thank all of the authors in this volume for their passion and commitment to telling the story of their research[1].

ARTICLES IN THE SPECIAL ISSUE

As previously mentioned, two of the articles in the special issue consider the intersection of motherhood and direct state-control, and both papers demonstrate the strength of integrating theoretical constructs across disciplinary differences in their analyses. Elizabeth A. Adams presents a quantitative assessment of mothers on probation or parole and their endorsement of the hegemonic mothering ideology, "intensive mothering" (Hays 1996). In "Intensive Parenting Ideologies and Risks for Recidivism Among Justice-Involved Mothers," the author empirically tests the relevance of the Intensive Parenting Attitudes Questionnaire (IPAQ) for justice-involved mothers. This scale, which has been validated on a general population of mothers, is designed to identify whether mothers agree with elements of intensive mothering, such as the belief that mothers are inherently better qualified to parent (essentialism). Hays (1996) argued that such values reflect a tenuous resistance to the allegedly rational values associated with late-stage capitalism, but they also put increased burdens on mothers for significant time and resource investments in their children. Here, the author considers whether the acceptance of these elements is significantly related to justice-involved mothers' risks for recidivism, which they aptly recognize are *a priori* complicated by motherhood-related economic and support limitations. Her results suggest some of mothers' intensive mothering beliefs are correlated with recidivism risks, a finding that calls into question correctional system programing that encourages intensive mothering beliefs in an effort to encourage better parenting.

Delving more deeply into the lived experiences of mothers under state-control, Ebonie Cunningham Stringer, in "Managing Motherhood: How Incarcerated Mothers Negotiate Maternal Role-Identities with their Children's Caregivers," asks how incarcerated mothers manage their mothering through their interactions with their children's caregivers. Cunningham Stringer uses group interviews to analyze how her respondents' strategic choices about authority, cooperation, and negotiation with the caregivers serve to prove the quality of their own mothering. Recognizing the liminality of mothering for many of the incarcerated mothers but also most of the mothers' commitment to their mother identities, Cunningham Stringer effectively considers how caregiver support of the women's maternal identities engenders those identities. Thus, caregivers not only may sustain the children of incarcerated mothers, they may also reinforce the maternal identities of the mothers.

Leah Iman Aniefuna, M. Amari Aniefuna, and Jason M. Williams shift our focus to Black women and mothers who are not officially under state-control, but who still experience the ramifications of state-control in their everyday lives in what the authors call "open-air prisons." "Creating and Undoing Legacies of Resilience: Black Women as Martyrs in the Black Community Under Oppressive Social Control" describes the effects of police violence on Black women and mothers, using interviews with 8 Black women following the murder of Freddie Gray in 2015.

[1]Thank you also to all of the presenters in the sessions I have organized on motherhood and crime at the American Society of Criminology annual meetings over the last few years who continue to broaden our understanding of how motherhood complicates, challenges and sometimes criminalizes the experiences of women. Finally, I would like to send out a special thanks to *Women & Criminal Justice* Editor Fran Bernat for her patience and professionalism as we pulled together this Special Issue.

Grounding their analyses in Critical Race Theory and Black Feminist Criminology, the authors explore how the trauma and violence of the women's interactions with police compound their vulnerability as Black mothers while increasing their children's trauma risks. The authors find that motherhood itself is used by the state to control and denigrate Black women, despite the relative invisibility of such trauma in the media. Yet the article also acknowledges the resilience of Black women and mothers as they turn to faith, creativity, community and education to survive, to mother their children, and to support each other.

"Discourses of Good Motherhood and the Policing of Young Parenthood" by Amber-Lee Varadi, Rebecca Raby, and Christine Tardif-Williams takes us outside of the criminal legal system and challenges us to consider the effects of criminalizing on young mothers. Describing their community-based participants' experiences inclusively as "policing," the authors invoke Foucault (1977/1995) to argue that judgments of others serve to regulate and discipline young mothers' behaviors. Just as Pasko (2017) argued that juvenile justice system actors seek to restrain girls' sexual and reproductive choices, here Varadi and her colleagues conclude that extra-institutional actors also judge young mothers. Further, ideologies of motherhood and pejorative discourses particularly targeted toward young mothers facilitate self-policing, even without the judgmental eyes of others, because of neoliberal understandings of responsibilization. Within this context, the young mothers' self-policing, such as avoiding interactions with strangers while critiquing the presumed judgments they would receive in such interactions, can be read as both an internalization of the negative discourses and an awareness of and resistance to proscriptions of how they should engage in mothering.

Finally, the last article in this Special Issue considers the issue of abortion while enhancing our discussion of state violence against women and mothers by considering efforts to manage abortion access across and through geopolitical locations. Lula Mecinska, Carolyne James & Kate Mukungu's article, "Criminalization of Women Accessing Abortion and Enforced Mobility within the European Union and United Kingdom," is a complex analysis of laws and regulations about abortion in the UK, Poland and Italy. In describing certain states' "outsourcing" of abortion, the authors unpack the un/intended construction of migration as a fraught strategy for women to circumvent punitive or restrictive laws in their home countries. The paper's in-depth multi-state analysis will be a valuable resource for scholars concerned with increasing restrictions on abortion internationally[2].

CONCLUDING THOUGHTS

This is a prime moment to talk about the importance of researching motherhood and reproductive justice[3]. The COVID-19 pandemic that has led to over 100,000 deaths in the United States (as of June 1, 2020), has disproportionately affected women and mothers. Incarcerated inmates who are pregnant are left to languish in prisons and jails with increasing rates of COVID-19 infections (Villarreal, 2020), resulting in at least one pregnant inmate death in Texas, Andrea Circle Bear (Shepherd, 2020). Ms. Circle Bear's story is particularly resonant for feminist criminologists, because she was in prison because of the War on Drugs—a war that has decimated communities of Color (see e.g. Alexander, 2012) and differentially impacted Women of Color (Bush-Baskette, 1998; Ritchie, 2017). Attacks on reproductive rights in the US have also accelerated during the pandemic, from access to abortion services (Cohen & Joffe, 2020; Lockwood, 2020) to the hospital exclusion of partners and/or doulas while women are in labor (Davis-Floyd et al., 2020).

---

[2]For a discussion of abortion politics in the United States and especially the criminalization of women's bodies in relation to abortion policies, see Michelle Goodwin (2019).

[3]I am, of course, referring to the understandings of reproductive justice put forward by the SisterSong Collective, cohesively discussed in Ross and Solinger (2017).

This state and medical violence is surrounded by enhanced expectations for mothers and mothering related to the closure of schools, the loss of jobs, and especially social distancing (O'Reilly, 2020). The unevenly distributed unpaid care burden for children, the elderly, and the ill has more severely tipped toward increased work for women, particularly within homes. How are we to make sense of mothering—both good and bad—during this era of near uninterrupted demand on mothers? In New York City, for instance, which has been hit severely by virus cases, illnesses and deaths, teachers and other school personnel are expected to continue to serve as mandatory reporters to identify children who may be victims of neglect and abuse (Carranza, 2020; Grench, 2020). This has led to parents facing economic challenges such as a lack of electronic or internet resources—perhaps even compounded by loss of their homes resulting in families living in a shelter (Grench, 2020)—to be reported to child services for "educational neglect" (Carranza, 2020).

Both feminist criminologists and motherhood scholars, and particularly those researchers working across these fields, are well-prepared to analyze whether COVID-19 has exacerbated the criminalization of mothers and pregnant individuals. I look forward to reading those articles.

REFERENCES

Alexander, M. (2012). *The new Jim Crow: Mass incarceration in the age of colorblindness*. The New Press.

Aniefuna L, Aniefuna M. A., & Williams, J. (2020). Creating and undoing legacies of resilience: Black women as martyrs in the Black community under oppressive social control. *Women & Criminal Justice*. https://doi.org/10.1080/08974454.2020.1752352

Bromwich, R. J. (2017). Still wearing scarlet? Discursive figures of the unfit mother as pervasive phantoms active in governing mothers through Ontario's child protection regime. In M. Hughes Miller, T. Hager, & R. J. Bromwich (Eds.), *Bad mothers: Regulations, representations, and resistance* (pp. 26–47). Demeter Press.

Bromwich, R. J. (2020). Formal governance of and by mothers: Mothers, public policy, and law. In L. O'Brien Hallstein, A. O'Reilly, & M. Vandenbeld Giles (Eds.), *The Routledge companion to motherhood* (pp. 429–441). Routledge.

Brown, M., & Bloom, B. (2009). Colonialism and carceral motherhood: Native Hawaiian families under corrections and child welfare control. *Feminist Criminology*, *4*(2), 151–169. https://doi.org/10.1177/1557085108325232

Burgess-Proctor, A. (2010). Looking back, looking ahead: Assessing contemporary feminist criminology. In J. H. Copes, & V. Topalli (Eds.), *Criminological theory: Readings and retrospectives* (pp. 431–443). McGraw-Hill.

Bush-Baskette, S. R. (1998). The war on drugs as a war on black women. In S. Miller (Ed.), *Crime control and women: feminist implications of criminal justice policy* (pp. 113–121). Sage Publications.

Carranza, R. A. (2020). *Child abuse and maltreatment prevention and intervention during remote learning and at the regional enrichment centers*. Memo from the NYC Department of Education. https://www.uft.org/sites/default/files/attachments/coronavirus-child-abuse-prevention.pdf

Chesler, P. (1991). *Mothers on trial: The battle for children and custody*. Chicago Review Press.

Chesney-Lind, M. (2017). Editorial: Policing women's bodies: Law, crime, sexuality, and reproduction. *Women & Criminal Justice*, *27*(1), 1–3. https://doi.org/10.1080/08974454.2017.1268014

Cohen, D. S., Joffe, C. (2020, March 25). Anti-choice politicians are using the coronavirus crisis to deny abortion rights. *Rolling Stone*. https://www.rollingstone.com/politics/political-commentary/anti-choice-politicians-are-using-the-coronavirus-crisis-to-deny-abortion-rights-973096/

Davis-Floyd, D., Gutschow, K., & Schwartz, D. A. (2020). Pregnancy, birth and the COVID-19 pandemic in the United States. *Medical Anthropology*. https://doi.org/10.1080/01459740.2020.1761804

Enos, S. (2001). *Mothering from the inside: Parenting in a women's prison*. State University of New York Press.

Feinman, C. (1992). *The criminalization of a woman's body*. Routledge.

Foucault, M. (1977/1995). *Discipline and punish: The birth of the prison* (2nd ed., A. Sheridan, Trans.). Vintage Books.

Goodwin, M. (2019). *Policing the* womb: *Invisible* women and the criminalization of motherhood. Cambridge University Press.

Grench, E. (2020, April 28). Parents expecting iPad deliveries got knock on door from child welfare workers. *The City*. https://www.thecity.nyc/education/2020/4/28/21247059/parents-expecting-ipad-deliveries-got-knock-on-door-from-child-welfare-workers

Hays, S. (1996). *The cultural contradictions of motherhood*. Yale University Press.

Hill Collins, P. (1990). *Black feminist thought: Knowledge, consciousness, and the politics of empowerment*. Routledge.

Hughes Miller, M. (2020). The governance of mothers. In L. O'Brien Hallstein, A. O'Reilly, & M. Vandenbeld Giles (Eds.), *The Routledge companion to motherhood* (pp. 451–461). Routledge.

Hughes Miller, M., Hager, T., & Bromwich, R. J. (2017). The bad mother in relief. In M. Hughes Miller, T. Hager, & R. J. Bromwich (Eds.), *Bad mothers: Regulations, representations, and resistance* (pp. 1–21). Demeter Press.

Kawash, S. (2011). New directions in motherhood studies. *Signs: Journal of Women in Culture and Society*, *36*(4), 969–1003. https://doi.org/10.1086/658637

Lerner, S. (2010). *War on moms: on life in a family-unfriendly nation*. Wiley.

Lockwood, A. (2020, May 28). UN experts urge US states to honor reproductive rights amid COVID-19 pandemic. *Jurist*. https://www.jurist.org/news/2020/05/un-experts-urge-us-states-to-honor-reproductive-rights-amid-covid-19-pandemic/

Mecinska, L., James, C. & Mukungu, K. (2020). Criminalization of women accessing abortion and enforced mobility within the European Union and United Kingdom. *Women & Criminal Justice*. https://doi.org/10.1080/08974454.2020.1758868

Michalsen, V. (2019). *Mothering and desistance in re-entry*. Routledge.

Minaker, J., & Hogeveen, B., eds. (2015). *Criminalized mothers, criminalizing mothering*. Demeter Press.

O'Reilly, A. (2016). *Matricentric feminism: Theory, activism, and practice*. Demeter Press.

O'Reilly, A. (2020). *Mothers are front-line workers: Care and crisis under COVID-19*. https://www.facebook.com/watch/live/?v=228788488392149&ref=watch_permalink

Pasko, L. (2017). Beyond confinement: The regulation of girl offenders' bodies, sexual choices, and behavior. *Women & Criminal Justice*, *27*(1), 4–20. https://doi.org/10.1080/08974454.2016.1259598

Potter, P. (2015). *Intersectionality and criminology: Disrupting and revolutionizing studies of crime*. Routledge.

Renzetti, C. (2018). Feminist theories. In W. S. DeKeseredy & M. Dragiewicz (Eds.), *Routledge handbook of critical criminology* (pp. 74–82). Routledge.

Rich, A. (1976). *Of woman born: Motherhood as experience and institution*. W.W. Norton.

Ritchie, A. (2017). *Invisible no more: Police violence against black women and women of color*. Beacon Press.

Roberts, D. E. (1997). *Killing the black body: Race, reproduction, and the meaning of liberty*. Vintage.

Ross, L., & Solinger, R. (2017). *Reproductive justice: An introduction*. University of California Press.

Rothman, B. K. (1989). *Recreating motherhood*. W.W. Norton.

Ruddick, S. (1995). *Maternal thinking: Toward a politics of peace*. Beacon Press.

Shepherd, K. (2020, April 4). Coronavirus kills its first female federal inmate weeks after she had an emergency C-section. *The Washington Post*. https://www.washingtonpost.com/nation/2020/04/29/pregnant-inmate-death-coronavirus/

Villarreal, A. (2020, May 22). Pregnant inmates languish in US prisons despite promises of release. *The Guardian*. https://www.theguardian.com/us-news/2020/may/22/us-prisons-pregnant-inmates-coronavirus-pandemic-release

Wong, G. (2012). Introduction. In G. Wong (Ed.), *Moms gone mad: Motherhood and madness, oppression and resistance*. Demeter Press.

Intensive Parenting Ideologies and Risks for Recidivism among Justice-Involved Mothers

Elizabeth A. Adams

ABSTRACT
Intensive parenting is the dominant parenting ideology in the United States, and it holds parents, especially mothers, accountable for the outcomes of their children, and urges them to expend extensive time and resources on child-rearing, even when such efforts compromise the parent's wellbeing. Research continuously highlights the harms associated with women's intensive parenting beliefs. This study employed factor analysis on the Intensive Parenting Attitudes Questionnaire to examine whether the resulting dimensions of intensive parenting related to risks for recidivism for 164 justice-involved mothers. Results indicated that their strong endorsement of essentialism (beliefs that mothers are uniquely qualified and responsible for child-rearing) and parenting that is all-consuming (beliefs that parenting requires great time and effort) were significantly associated with multiple risks for recidivism. The findings clarify how specific intensive parenting beliefs factor into mothers' risks for recidivism and suggest the importance of not encouraging these beliefs in correctional settings.

INTRODUCTION

Criminal justice research and policy has largely focused on addressing men's needs due to their greater representation in correctional populations (Bloom et al., 2004; Opsal, 2009). However, the number of justice-involved women in the United States has risen dramatically in the aftermath of the war on drugs and tough on crime policies (Bloom et al., 2004; Ferraro & Moe, 2003; Mauer et al., 1999; Opsal, 2009; Petersilia, 2003). Between 1995 and 2015 the number of women supervised in the community doubled from 575,631 to 1,056,700, while men supervised in the community grew by half that rate (Bureau of Justice Statistics, 1997; Kaeble & Bonczar, 2016). Given the huge increase in the population of justice-involved women, scholars have emphasized the need for ongoing research on justice-involved women's experiences. Existing research highlights how gender-specific disadvantages uniquely impact women's initial offending (Belknap, 2014; Bloom et al., 2003; Daly & Chesney-Lind, 1988; Morash, 2010) and recidivism (Garcia, 2016; Van Voorhis, 2012; Van Voorhis et al., 2010, 2012, 2013). Disadvantages that are more prevalent among justice-involved women compared to their male counterparts include trauma stemming from physical and sexual abuse (Payne et al., 2005), substance abuse (Fedock et al., 2013; Morash, 2010; Neff & Waite, 2007; Office of National Drug Control Policy, 2013), mental illness (Belknap & Holsinger, 2006; Bloom et al., 2003; Kessler, 1998; Lynch et al., 2014; Peters et al., 1997), as well as economic and social marginalization (Greenfeld & Snell, 1999; Uggen & Kruttschnitt, 1998).

Compared to justice-involved men, parenting responsibilities also serve a more prominent role in justice-involved women's risks for recidivism (Giordano, 2010; Seng & Lurigio, 2005), and such responsibilities tend to complicate or be complicated by other challenges mothers face on supervision (Arditti & Few, 2008; Brown & Bloom, 2009; Robison & Hughes Miller, 2016). It is reasonable that parenting is a central concern among justice-involved women since they are typically single parents (Salisbury & Van Voorhis, 2009; The Sentencing Project, 2012). Also, compared to fathers, mothers are more likely to be their children's primary caregiver prior to incarceration, and incarcerated mothers are two times more likely than fathers to rely on caregivers (e.g., grandparents and the foster care system) aside from the other biological parent (Glaze & Maruschak, 2008). Such alternative placements can provoke concern for children's safety and development, as well as for the parent's ability to regain relationships with and custody of children (Brown & Bloom, 2009; Muhammad, 2012).

Feminist researchers have argued that women's unique risks for recidivism are the result of gendered norms which specify obligations and opportunities for women, impeding their ability to achieve equality with men in social and economic spheres of society (Bloom et al., 2004; Douglas & Michaels, 2004; Pollack, 2007). These norms prescribe that females be caring, polite, and submissive (Collins, 2009; West & Zimmerman, 1987). However, by the nature of the labels of "criminals" and "addicts," justice-involved women violate these expectations (Douglas & Michaels, 2004; Golden, 2005). Justice-involved mothers are judged especially severely as they are also seen as violating gendered expectations of "good mothers" (Granja et al., 2015; Robison & Hughes Miller, 2016) who put children's needs before their own and who dedicate boundless attention and resources to child-rearing (Hays, 1996). Politicians and media outlets have emboldened public scrutiny of mothers struggling with addiction and poverty by using scientifically misconstrued research that portrays them as welfare abusers and bad mothers (Belknap, 2014; Douglas & Michaels, 2004). As a result of this rhetoric, parenting is commonly considered to be the source and solution of some of the country's most crucial problems, such as educational deficits and delinquency (Collins, 2009; Douglas & Michaels, 2004; Golden, 2005).

These norms are reflected through the dominant parenting ideology in the United States, intensive parenting, which emphasizes the vital role of mothers in child-rearing as well as their need to expend extensive time and resources to raise children as successful members of society (Hays, 1996; Newman & Henderson, 2014; Rizzo, Schiffrin, & Liss, 2013; Wall, 2010). Qualitative research on intensive parenting has demonstrated how women are subjected to intensive parenting expectations and also commonly subscribe to this belief system regardless of the resources available for mothers to meet these expectations (Collins, 2009; Granja et al., 2015; Hays, 1996; Romagnoli & Wall, 2012). Research also indicates that being held to and subscribing to intensive parenting beliefs can lead to consequences for women such as reductions in life satisfaction and self-efficacy, as well as increases in stress, guilt, and anxiety (Henderson et al., 2016; Newman & Henderson, 2014; Rizzo et al., 2013; Wall, 2010).

Harms associated with intensive parenting beliefs may be more profound for mothers who face additional obstacles to meeting expectations, such as obstacles faced by single, low-income, mothers under correctional control (Granja et al., 2015; Hays, 1996; Romagnoli & Wall, 2012). Justice-involved mothers' perceptions of failures in parenting may lead to guilt or shame and in turn prompt them to develop impractical goals to help them repair their maternal identity and their relationships with their children (Brown & Bloom, 2009; Ferraro & Moe, 2003; Opsal, 2009). Justice-involved mothers' exhaustive attempts to achieve idealistic parenting goals can lead them to disregard their personal needs like treatment for mental health issues and addiction (Hagan & Dinovitzer, 1999) and result in their continued use of harmful coping mechanisms (Brown & Bloom, 2009; Ferraro & Moe, 2003; Opsal, 2009, 2015).

Although existing research offers insight on the harms associated with intensive parenting beliefs, most of this research is qualitative, and the few quantitative studies on this subject have focused on intensive parenting beliefs and consequences for middle and upper-class, White women (Henderson et al., 2016; Liss et al., 2013; Rizzo et al., 2013). The current study used the Intensive Parenting Attitudes Questionnaire (IPAQ), which was developed and validated by social psychologists (Liss et al., 2013), to examine justice-involved mothers' subscription to dimensions of intensive parenting. The research also provided a quantitative exploration of the ways in which intensive parenting beliefs relate to justice-involved mothers' risks for recidivism. The results are relevant to improving correctional practices and raising practitioner awareness of the potential consequences of employing intensive parenting rhetoric in interactions with clients.

LITERATURE REVIEW

Justice-Involved Women's Risks for Recidivism and Parenting Problems

To better understand the impact of intensive parenting beliefs on mothers, it is imperative to identify the risks for recidivism found in studies on justice-involved women. Compared to men, substance abuse and some forms of mental illness are more common risks for women's recidivism (Belknap & Holsinger, 2006; Bloom et al., 2003; Kessler, 1998; Peters et al., 1997). Mental health concerns that are more salient predictors of women's recidivism include depression, anxiety, and feelings of anger and hostility, as well as low levels of self-efficacy (Van Voorhis, 2012; Van Voorhis et al., 2010, 2012, 2013). Research that has included women has also indicated that life satisfaction is an important indicator of abstinence from drug use and desistance from antisocial behavior (Laudet, 2011; Laudet et al., 2009).

Women's risks for recidivism are compounded for mothers who are responsible for caring for and protecting minor children, particularly when they lack necessary assistance and resources to do so (Greene et al., 2000). Since justice-involved mothers are often single parents, those that have custody of their children can be consumed by childcare responsibilities (Salisbury & Van Voorhis, 2009; The Sentencing Project, 2012). Managing parenting problems also may be particularly problematic for justice-involved women because research indicates they are less able to rely on others for social support compared to justice-involved men (Mallik-Kane & Visher, 2008). Women's responsibilities for children as single parents and their lack of support from others diminishes their prospects for employment, which in turn increases the gendered division of labor, thereby exacerbating the marginalization of women (Brown & Bloom, 2009; Ferraro & Moe, 2003). Parenting is likely more stressful for mothers rearing children with behavioral problems that require mothers to expend additional effort in child-rearing, and that contribute to mothers' frustration when their efforts seem to be ineffective (Giordano, 2010; McLoyd, 1990). Narrative accounts of justice-involved mothers indicate that many of them feel overwhelmed by parenting, so they experience heightened depression, mental illness and substance use (Arditti & Few, 2008; Ferraro & Moe, 2003; Greene et al., 2000). Quantitative research has also shown that parenting stress is associated with justice-involved mothers' substance use and increased recidivism (Adams et al., 2017; Van Voorhis et al., 2012, 2013).

Concerns about children's wellbeing and a mother's maternal identity are amplified during periods of separation brought on by incarceration, residential treatment and custody loss, which may also impact a mother's ability to cope while on supervision (Arditti & Few, 2008; Baker & Carson, 1999; Baunach, 1985; Grella & Greenwell, 2006; Michalsen, 2011; Richie, 2001). Justice-involved mothers fighting to maintain or gain custody of their children need to put effort into proving to others that they are good mothers, because Child Protective Services (CPS) frequently surveils them, and these investigations often involve their supervision agents' assessment of their suitability as mothers (Brown & Bloom, 2009; Morash, 2010). Individuals on supervision are subject to a variety of time-consuming and challenging requirements including regular meetings with agents, routine drug testing, mental health services, self-help groups, community service, full-time employment, gaining educational accreditation, and paying fees (O'Brien, 2001; Opsal, 2009). Meeting these extensive requirements is particularly difficult for mothers who are subject to parent-related requirements and who have child-care responsibilities (Brown & Bloom, 2009; Opsal, 2009; Robison & Hughes Miller, 2016).

Justice-involved mothers face additional obstacles to meeting these requirements as they often lack access to necessary resources—such as income, transportation and social support—to complete these tasks (Mallik-Kane & Visher, 2008; Northcutt-Bohmert, 2016; Salisbury & Van Voorhis, 2009). The emotional penalties mothers face as they struggle to successfully complete supervision and meet intensive parenting expectations could explain why stigma is more influential in women's desistance in comparison to men's (Uggen & Kruttschnitt, 1998). To properly ground this study on the impacts of intensive parenting beliefs for justice involved mothers, it is crucial to review the research on intensive parenting.

Consequences of Intensive Parenting Ideologies

In qualitative research on mothers, Hays (1996) developed the term "intensive parenting" to refer to the widespread expectations that mothers should dedicate extensive time and resources to child-rearing. The expectations that mothers in her study discussed included recognizing the ways to properly raise children during different developmental periods, performing difficult tasks, and buying costly products and services to ensure children's prosperity. The mothers also said they were commonly encouraged to seek expert knowledge about parenting through various sources (e.g. books, magazines, newsletters, parenting classes) that claimed to offer information on the best ways to raise children. They reported that these sources sometimes offered contradictory and ambiguous advice, but that most emphasized the importance of spending time with children and stimulating children throughout their development. Hays (1996) also found that the majority of the mothers believed parenting should be the most fulfilling role in life and that women are uniquely qualified and accountable for raising their children properly. Intensive parenting expectations have become increasingly popular and demanding due to society's growing concern about child development and the media's fixation on the best ways to parent and on the consequences of improper parenting practices (Douglas & Michaels, 2004; Hays, 1996; Romagnoli & Wall, 2012; Wall, 2010).

Researchers indicate that intensive parenting is the dominant parenting ideology in the United States and that this belief system disregards the increase of female-headed, single parent households as well as women's increased participation in the labor force (Collins, 2009; Damaske, 2013; Douglas & Michaels, 2004; Hays, 1996; Henderson et al., 2016; Newman & Henderson, 2014; Rizzo et al., 2013; Romagnoli & Wall, 2012; Wall, 2010). Specifically, intensive parenting expectations designate mothers as the primary caregivers for their children despite the increasing need for women to work to provide for their families. These paradoxical expectations encourage mothers to choose between employment and assuming full time caregiving responsibilities, and both choices can generate ramifications for mothers like financial stress and feelings of guilt (Douglas & Michaels, 2004; Hays, 1996; Henderson et al., 2016). Mothers who need to work and who also strongly subscribe to intensive parenting may push themselves to destructive levels of emotional and physical exhaustion as they struggle to perform both functions. Qualitative studies have shown how women's subscription to intensive parenting can limit their success in other aspects of life and reduce their wellbeing because of exhaustive efforts or negative feelings resulting from their perceptions of failure (Collins, 2009; Douglas & Michaels, 2004; Wall, 2010). When paired with social and economic adversity, intensive parenting policies can lead mothers to enact particularly strenuous parenting strategies to effectively raise children (Collins, 2009; Jarrett, 1999).

For example, Jarrett (1999) found that Black single mothers who resided in dangerous neighborhoods performed rigorous tasks to raise children (i.e. isolating themselves and their children, escorting children to their activities, intensely monitoring their children's associates, and providing children with at-home learning activities to supplement inadequate public schooling in their communities). Jarrett (1999) also concluded that these tasks limited the mothers' personal opportunities and wellbeing, as well as their ability to gain employment to provide for themselves and their children. Other research indicates that adversity faced by women with limited opportunities can lead mothers to pursue alternative parenting ideologies, especially women of color who often have backgrounds and opportunities that are inconsistent with the White, middle class experiences that shape intensive parenting expectations (Collins, 2009). Specifically, adversity has prompted mothers to reframe prevailing intensive parenting expectations by redefining what it means to be a "good mother" given their circumstances. Women can also actively resist the dominant ideology by enacting practices that counter essentialist beliefs which conflict with their need to work to support children, often as single mothers. For instance, Collins (2009) described how Black mothers' heightened need to work to support their families can lead them to seek assistance from "othermothers," which refers to females in their families or communities who serve as supplementary or primary caregivers for their children. Although these practices are respected within Black communities because they can advance community prosperity, alternative parenting pursuits are undermined by policies that regulate parental liability and that constrain resources available to compensate caregivers (Collins, 2009).

Studies have also indicated that institutions can serve to support or reject the dominant intensive parenting ideology (LaBorde, 2009; Newman & Henderson, 2014; Wall, 2010). Programs that include intensive parenting rhetoric have been found to be ineffective, dissatisfying, and even harmful, especially for parents who subscribe to, but are incapable of fulfilling expectations. For instance, in a study of the impact of an intensive parenting intervention aimed at enhancing parental responsibility for children's educational success, Wall (2010) found that mothers performed prescribed behaviors, but also experienced increased guilt, stress and anxiety. In an ethnographic examination of a parenting program, Newman and Henderson (2014) identified intensive parenting rhetoric reflecting essentialist assumptions that mothers are the most significant determinant of children's wellbeing, and that they must make large sacrifices for their children. Mothers attending this program reported decreased self-fulfillment and well-being and increased guilt based on their inability to meet program expectations. Overall, the research suggests that being held to and subscribing to intensive parenting beliefs can be harmful for mothers (Henderson et al., 2016; Newman & Henderson, 2014; Rizzo et al., 2013; Wall, 2010).

Women who strongly subscribe to intensive parenting, but also face barriers to achieving intensive parenting, such as those faced by justice-involved mothers (e.g. incarceration, custody issues, limited resources) may develop distorted perceptions of their capabilities. These distortions may lead to disappointments that generate additional stress and damage to their maternal identity (Granja et al., 2015). Research on parenting beliefs using discourse analysis has shown that low-income women and justice-involved women subscribe to aspects of intensive parenting even though they are rooted in White, middle class society (Granja et al., 2015; Hays, 1996; Romagnoli & Wall, 2012). The research on justice-involved mothers suggests that the consequences of intensive parenting are amplified for them due to their limited access to resources that would assist them in meeting such expectations, and because of stigma that can harm their maternal identity and limit their contact with children (Granja et al., 2015). Mothers struggling with poverty and addiction may be distinctly encumbered by intensive parenting rhetoric since they are often targeted by CPS and in turn are required to attend parenting programs to maintain or gain desired custody (Collins, 2009; LaBorde, 2009). Research on the experiences of mothers on community supervision has pointed to intensive parenting expectations as an explanation for the challenges and negative outcomes of mothers struggling to meet parenting goals while also attempting to manage supervision requirements, CPS involvement, and addressing their personal needs (Brown & Bloom, 2009; Ferraro & Moe, 2003; Opsal, 2009, 2015; Robison & Hughes Miller, 2016). Though existing research is valuable in terms of identifying how being subject to expectations and subscribing to intensive parenting ideologies can lead to negative consequences for some women, this research is primarily qualitative. Therefore, it is unclear whether particular dimensions of intensive parenting are significant predictors of negative outcomes for mothers in conflict with the law.

To enable quantitative assessment of intensive parenting beliefs, Liss et al. (2013) designed and validated the IPAQ to evaluate the statistical dimensions and correlates of intensive parenting beliefs. They developed the IPAQ based on questions they created that reflected common themes found in existing qualitative research on intensive parenting (Hays, 1996; Wall, 2010). After conducting exploratory factor analysis (EFA) and a confirmatory factor analysis (CFA) they found that the intensive parenting beliefs of their sample of women were reflected by five distinct dimensions: essentialism (women are inherently qualified and responsible for caregiving); all-consuming (parenting should be difficult and require great time and effort); stimulation (parents should stimulate children as they develop); child-centered (parents should make sacrifices for children); and fulfillment (parenting should be fulfilling) (Liss et al., 2013). In a follow-up study, they analyzed the relationship between intensive parenting beliefs and women's mental health. They found that mothers with stronger essentialist beliefs had lower life satisfaction, and that mothers with stronger all-consuming beliefs had higher levels of stress and depression (Rizzo et al., 2013). Therefore, justice-involved mothers' essentialist and all-consuming beliefs may exhibit stronger correlations with their risks for recidivism compared to the other dimensions.

RESEARCH FOCUS

To shed light on the intensive parenting beliefs of justice-involved mothers, the current study used EFA and CFA to examine whether the IPAQ captured intensive parenting beliefs of women who had minor children while on probation or parole. Then significant dimensions that were identified were examined in relation to mothers' risks for recidivism. The following research questions guided this study:

1. Are dimensions of intensive parenting beliefs identified for justice-involved mothers using the IPAQ? If so, which ones?
2. Do these dimensions differ between the current sample of justice-involved mothers and the original sample of mothers from the general population? If so, how?
3. Do these dimensions of intensive parenting relate to risks for recidivism for justice-involved mothers?

METHODOLOGY

Sampling and Participants

The data were drawn from a longitudinal study of 402 women on probation or parole in Michigan for a felony crime. Because substance-involved women represent the largest subsection of justice-involved women (Langan & Pelissier, 2001; Morash, 2010), only women with an indication of previous or current involvement with alcohol or drugs were sampled. The women on supervision were selected from the caseloads of 73 supervision agents recruited from 16 counties within an hour and a half drive from the study's office. The final sample of agents included at least one agent in each of the 16 counties. These counties included 68.5 percent of the state population in 2011, when the study began, and a variety of urban, suburban, and rural locations.

The available data are from five interviews with women who started supervision in 2011 or 2012. The current study is based on quantitative data from the fifth interview which took place roughly five years after the first interview. The fifth interview was conducted over the phone with 64.7 percent of the initial sample ($n = 260$). A comparison of participants from the fifth interview and the initial sample of 402 indicated they did not significantly differ on criminal history or other risks for recidivism that may be relevant to the current study. At the first interview 208 women had minor children, and at the fifth interview the number of women with minor children reduced to 173. Women who became parents after supervision ended were excluded from the subsample because the aim of this study was to understand the intensive parenting beliefs of women who experienced community supervision as mothers. The final subsample includes 164 women who were mothers to minor children while under supervision, and who participated in the fifth interview.

At the first interview the average age of the mothers in this analysis was just over 31 years old ($M = 31.88$, $SD = 8.40$, range = 19 – 59). Most of the mothers identified as White ($n = 83$, 50.6%), or Black ($n = 59$, 36.0%), a small number reported being Native American ($n = 2$, 1.22%), or Pacific Islander ($n = 1$, 0.6%), and some reported being multiracial ($n = 19$, 11.6%). A higher proportion of the women ($n = 134$, 81.7%) were on probation compared to parole ($n = 30$, 18.3%). At the fifth interview most women reported having a high school diploma or GED ($n = 131$, 80.0%), but fewer reported attending some college or post high school classes ($n = 91$, 55.5%), and only two of the women reported that they received a college degree ($n = 2$, 1.2%). Though many women reported having job certificates ($n = 76$, 46.3%), and educational and vocational career plans ($n = 113$, 68.9%), almost half reported being unable to work due to school, family responsibilities, or health problems, ($n = 53$, 32.3%) or being unemployed and able to work ($n = 40$, 24.4%). Less than a quarter of the women indicated they had part time ($n = 31$, 18.9%) or full-time employment ($n = 41$, 25.0%). Most of the women also reported making less than $10,000 per year ($n = 102$, 62.2%). A small portion reported being married ($n = 27$, 16.5%), and the majority reported being single parents ($n = 90$, 54.9%). Since supervision began women reported having 1–5 children ($M = 2.13$) under 18, and their children's ages ranged from 0–22 with an average age of 10.87 at the fifth interview.

Measurement

Intensive Parenting Beliefs

To examine intensive parenting beliefs of justice-involved mothers in relation to their risks for recidivism, the IPAQ was incorporated into the fifth interview. As is best practice in creating a scale based on qualitative research (Creswell & Plano Clark, 2011; DeVellis, 1991), Liss et al. (2013) used the language of participants from prior qualitative research to form a large number of items reflective of themes. Response options ranged from strongly disagree = 1 to strongly agree = 6. After conducting the 56-item survey Liss et al. (2013) performed an EFA with 318 mothers and found that 32 items reflective of intensive parenting beliefs loaded on five factors: essentialism, all-consuming, stimulation, child-centered, and fulfillment. All of the factors met acceptable levels of reliability based on Cronbach's alpha scores above .60 (Cronbach, 1951).

Risks for Recidivism

Risks for recidivism assessed in this study included current substance use, depression and anxiety, anger and hostility, low self-efficacy, low life satisfaction, and parenting stress. Measures of current substance use, depression and anxiety, and anger and hostility were developed as part of the Women's Risk/Needs Assessment (WRNA, Van Voorhis, 2012). The WRNA scale items have the response options, yes = 1, no = 0. Current substance use was based on seven questions such as,

"Are you currently using?" and "Do you currently have any feelings that you need to use drugs first thing in the morning?" ($M = .82$, $SD = 1.29$, range = $0 - 6$, Cronbach's alpha = .71). Depression and anxiety were measured by six questions regarding women's affirmative responses to recent experiences such as, "Having trouble sleeping because you are too worried about things?" ($M = 2.18$, $SD = 2.11$, range = $0 - 6$, Cronbach's alpha = .83). A combined measure of anger and hostility was measured by women's responses to three questions like, "In recent months, do you have trouble controlling your temper when you get upset?" ($M = 1.01$, $SD = 1.09$, range = $0 - 3$, Cronbach's alpha = .64). Sherer and colleague's (1982) self-efficacy scale was used. An example of the 17 items, which had response options ranging from seldom/never = 0 to often = 2, is "Do you feel capable of dealing with most problems that come up in life?" ($M = 7.00$, $SD = 34.00$, range = $7 - 34$, Cronbach's Alpha = .87). Life satisfaction was measured through the sum across five items from the life satisfaction scale developed by Diener and colleagues (Diener et al., 1985; Pavot & Diener, 1993). The response options range from 1 = strongly disagree to 7 = strongly agree. An example is, "In most ways my life is close to my ideal" ($M = 19.85$, $SD = 7.74$, range = $5 - 35$, Cronbach's alpha = .85).

One risk for recidivism, parenting stress (Van Voorhis, 2012), specifically pertained to features of motherhood. Parenting stress was examined through 12 items with four response options ranging from 1 = strongly disagree to 4 = strongly agree. Women were asked to consider their life with their children when they responded to the questions, and example items include, "Raising children is harder than I expected" and "Sometimes I feel like running away" ($M = 16.47$, $SD = 5.55$, range = $2 - 37$, Cronbach's alpha = .80).

Analytic Strategy

The EFA and CFA in the current study were conducted using Mplus software (Muthén & Muthén, 1998-2017). First an EFA employing Maximum Likelihood Estimation and Varimax Rotation was conducted to determine the appropriate number of dimensions as well as to identify items to retain in the scales. The appropriate number of factors was guided by the a priori idea about the factor structure based on the IPAQ, as well as an examination of the number of eigenvalues above one based on the Kaiser criterion (Kaiser, 1958), and the scree plot from the EFA (Beavers et al., 2013; Costello & Osborne, 2005). Results from the EFA were examined to identify items to retain in the CFA based on loadings above .40 and cross-loadings below .25 (Tabachnick & Fidell, 2001).

To examine the fit of the model identified during the EFA, CFA results for the reduced model were compared with CFA results for the original set of 32 items that were set to load on their expected factors based on the IPAQ (Liss et al., 2013). The model was examined in comparison to the full model for model fit based on Chi-square test results and indices of approximate fit available through CFA in MPlus (i.e. AIC, BIC, CFI, RMSEA, SRMR). In CFA, a non-significant chi-square statistic ($p > .05$) indicates that the model is interpretable (Raykov & Marcoulides, 2006). When comparing models, the AIC and BIC should be lower in a well-fitting reduced model compared to the full model (Schreiber et al., 2006). Also, a model with a good fit is indicated by a CFI close to one (above .95) (Schermelleh-Engel et al., 2003), a RMSEA value below .06 (Bentler, 1995), and an SRMR value less than .05 (Hu & Bentler, 1995).

After factor analysis, normality of the scales was assessed with criteria for a relatively normal distribution between -1 and $+1$ (George & Mallery, 2010) and acceptable levels of internal consistency based on Cronbach's alpha scores above .60 (Cronbach, 1951; Vaske, 2008). Bivariate correlations were employed to examine the associations between the dimensions of intensive parenting that exhibited adequate normality and internal consistency and the mothers' risks for recidivism (i.e. current substance use, depression and anxiety, anger and hostility, low self-efficacy, low life satisfaction, and parenting stress).

Table 1. Factor loadings for the two-factor model.

Items retained from the IPAQ		Factor 1: Esstentialism	Factor 2: All-consuming
IP2.	Although fathers may mean well, they generally are not as good at parenting as mothers	**.641**	.097
IP3.	Men do not naturally know what to do with children	**.730**	.194
IP4.	Both fathers and mothers are equally able to care for children (Rev)	**.641**	.218
IP5.	Women are not necessarily better parents than men (Rev)	**.469**	.110
IP6.	Although fathers are important, ultimately children need mothers more	**.457**	−.007
IP8.	Ultimately, it is the mother who is responsible for how her child turns out	**.575**	.064
IP22.	Mothers never get a mental break from their children, even when they are physically apart	.109	**.573**
IP23.	Parenting is exhausting	.199	**.532**
IP24.	It is harder to be a good mother than to be a corporate executive	030	**.519**
IP25.	Being a parent means never having time for oneself	.164	**.670**

The items in bold exhibited loadings for the factor greater than .40 and cross-loadings with other factors below .25.

RESULTS

Intensive Parenting Beliefs of Justice-Involved Mothers

Though 11 dimensions of intensive parenting beliefs produced eigenvalues over one, an examination of the scree plot indicated that a three-factor solution was more tenable. To ascertain whether three factors best represented the data, additional EFAs forcing 2, 3, 4, and 5 factor solutions were examined. Unlike the original study which identified a five-factor solution (Liss et al., 2013), the results from the EFAs in this study indicated that a three-factor solution was a better fit to the data based on eigenvalues and more consistent item loadings on the appropriate factors from the IPAQ. After the elimination of items that warranted removal, 14 items remained and loaded on three of the five dimensions of intensive parenting (i.e. essentialism, all-consuming, stimulation).

The CFA for the 32 items for the five-factor model ($\chi^2(454) = 664.327$, $p < .001$; CFI = .745; RMSEA = .053; SRMR = .080; AIC = 18456.017; BIC = 18785.247) was compared to the more tenable three-factor model. The three-factor model with 14 items was far superior to the full model as the Chi-square results could be interpreted and the approximate fit statistics were within acceptable ranges indicating a good fit ($\chi^2(62) = 71.112$, $p = .200$; CFI = .974; RMSEA = .030; SRMR = .052; AIC = 6464.094; BIC = 6594.288).

Normality and internal reliability were assessed for the revised dimensions from the three-factor model: essentialism ($M = 15.17$, $SD = 5.34$, range $= 6 - 30$, $Skewness = 0.68$, $Kurtosis = 0.06$, Cronbach's Alpha = .71), stimulation ($M = 15.51$, $SD = 1.73$, range $= 11 - 18$, $Skewness = -0.36$, $Kurtosis = -0.50$, Cronbach's Alpha = .13), and all-consuming ($M = 15.53$, $SD = 4.37$, range $= 5 - 24$, $Skewness = -0.046$, $Kurtosis = -0.68$, Cronbach's Alpha = .67). Skewness and kurtosis were within acceptable limits for all three dimensions, but only essentialism and all-consuming exhibited acceptable levels of internal consistency. The low level of internal consistency for stimulation may be due to the limited number of items that fit within the dimension for justice-involved mothers in this sample (Brown, 2009). Therefore, stimulation was not considered in the correlational analysis and the EFA and CFA were reproduced to ensure that the two-factor solution was a good fit for the data. The results for the two-factor model exhibited a good fit, and

Table 2. Correlations among dimensions of intensive parenting and risks for recidivism.

Risks for recidivism	Essentialism	All-consuming
Current substance use	.014	.099
Depression and anxiety	.090	.271**
Anger and hostility	.073	.211**
Self-efficacy	−.160*	−.280**
Life satisfaction	−.034	.109
Parenting stress	.219**	.324**

*$p < .05$, **$p < .01$.

the smaller AIC and BIC indicated that when the items for stimulation were removed the model fit was improved ($\chi 2(34) = 43.448$, $p = .129$; CFI = .968; RMSEA = .041; SRMR = .049; AIC = 5623.488; and BIC = 5719.584). Table 1 displays the loadings and cross loadings for the final two-factor model.

Correlational Analysis

The correlations among the dimensions of intensive parenting beliefs and risks for recidivism are listed on Table 2. The dimensions of essentialism and all-consuming exhibited significant positive associations with parenting stress and significant negative associations with self-efficacy. This indicates that mothers who more strongly endorsed these beliefs also had higher levels of parenting stress and lower levels of self-efficacy. The dimension reflecting the belief that parenting is all-consuming also exhibited significant positive relationships with the mothers' depression and anxiety as well as their anger and hostility. Like the original study on a general sample of women, this study identified essentialism and all-consuming beliefs as qualities of intensive parenting that are potentially harmful based on their significant associations with lower levels of psychological wellbeing.

DISCUSSION

The findings indicate that the IPAQ is useful for identifying some dimensions of intensive parenting for justice-involved mothers. The results also provide insight into areas that the IPAQ could be improved to better assess dimensions of intensive parenting that should be considered for justice-involved mothers. In addition, this study explicated the relationships between mothers' risks for recidivism and their endorsement of the two dimensions of intensive parenting that were identified in the factor analyses (e.g. essentialism, all-consuming). The EFA and CFA were used to address the first and second research questions, "Are dimensions of intensive parenting beliefs identified for justice-involved mothers using the IPAQ? If so, which ones?" and "Do these dimensions differ between the current sample of justice-involved mothers and the original sample of mothers from the general population? If so, how?" The results indicate that several items in the IPAQ captured intensive parenting beliefs of justice-involved mothers through two separate dimensions including essentialism and all-consuming. However, some items that did not fit well for the dimensions of essentialism and all-consuming, and the items for stimulation, fulfillment, and child-centered were omitted from this study because they did not form reliable scales. The discrepancies could be due to differences in the expectations, values, resources, and experiences of mothers in general populations in comparison to justice-involved mothers. These differences could emerge based on the unique experiences mothers have due to justice-system involvement as well as from the economic and social marginalization they often face (Collins, 2009; Granja et al., 2015; Robison & Hughes Miller, 2016), particularly since almost half of the justice-involved women in the sample identified as women of color The mixed support for the IPAQ in this quantitative analysis complement qualitative research findings indicating that justice-involved mothers value tenets of intensive parenting but that they can also adjust their definitions and performances of intensive parenting to fit their situations and reduce negative feelings from their perceived inability to engage in intensive parenting (Granja et al., 2015; Robison & Hughes Miller, 2016).

Essentialism

For essentialism, two items did not fit in the scale and these items pertained to beliefs in the limitations of men's abilities as parents rather than beliefs in the unique abilities and responsibilities of women as parents that were targeted by five of the six items retained in the scale. The fact that these eight items loaded together for the original sample of women from the general population but not for the current sample of justice involved mothers suggests that justice-involved mothers may not strongly connect these two ideas about parenting abilities and sex. This could be due to justice-involved mothers' experiences relying on the father of their children or other men to assist or take full responsibility for parenting due to the mothers' struggles with addiction, mental illness, and justice-system involvement. However, given justice-involved mothers' limited ability to rely on their children's fathers for childcare (Glaze & Maruschak, 2008; Salisbury & Van Voorhis, 2009; The Sentencing Project, 2012), additional items reflecting the limitations of men's skills and responsibilities for child-rearing may reflect a separate but meaningful dimension of intensive parenting that uniquely impacts justice-involved mothers.

All-Consuming

Two items did not fit well and were omitted from the all-consuming scale. One exhibited a low loading for the justice-involved mothers in this sample but exhibited a high loading for the general sample of mothers from the original study. This item reflected the extent to which women believed that "parenting is the most demanding job in the world." Given that the majority of mothers in the sample were single mothers with limited education, their experiences working multiple, possibly labor intensive, jobs or managing without employment may make this statement inconsistent with their experiences. The other item was removed from the all-consuming scale because it had a significant cross-loading with essentialism. This may be because the wording focused on *mothers*, "To be an effective mother, a woman must possess wide-ranging skills." When developing items for a multidimensional scale, items should be made unique enough so that multiple dimensions are not tapped by a single item (Tabachnick & Fidell, 2001).

In addition, the 32 items from the IPAQ did not include items reflecting beliefs that parents should expend financial resources on children, and this was discussed at length in prior research on intensive parenting (Hays, 1996; LaBorde, 2009; Newman & Henderson, 2014). Items tapping into beliefs that parents need to expend financial resources to properly raise children could load with items reflecting all-consuming parenting, but these items could represent a separate dimension of intensive parenting. Since such expectations and beliefs could influence or be influenced by women's marginalization (Collins, 2009; LaBorde, 2009), it is important to consider this theme in research on justice-involved mothers. Items that pertain to women's need to allocate limited resources to child-rearing should also be included, because they may illuminate the unique ways in which mothers with limited resources experience intensive parenting and how they adapt to meet intensive parenting expectations despite their limited resources.

Stimulation

Stimulation was not a reliable scale in the current study, but the two items regarding the importance of educating and stimulating children as they develop that loaded together could be included in a revised scale aimed at understanding justice-involved mothers' beliefs. These items included, "It is important for children to be involved in classes, lessons and activities that engage and stimulate them" and "Parents should begin providing intellectual stimulation for their children prenatally, such as reading to them or playing classical music." The other item that loaded with stimulation was reversed, "Children are likely to grow up healthy and happy without much intervention from their parents." This item pertains to beliefs that parents are responsible for their children's outcomes, and this may represent a separate dimension of intensive parenting. Mothers may feel the need to protect children from risks when they live in dangerous neighborhoods (Cobbina et al., 2014; Jarrett, 1999), and justice-involved women often reside in dangerous and resource deprived communities. Therefore, justice-involved mothers' beliefs in a parent's responsibility to protect children from harm may denote another important method of intensive parenting that is distinct from stimulation and that is not prominent for those in the general population. An additional aspect that the original authors (Liss et al., 2013) tied to stimulation was the importance of following expert advice, but the one item that reflected this belief did not load well into the model for this study. More items reflecting the belief in the importance of seeking and following expert advice should be incorporated, as this may exhibit an additional dimension of intensive parenting. Justice-involved women's beliefs in the importance of expert advice regarding parenting is vital to understand since they are more likely to be classified as risks to their children due to their struggles with poverty and addiction (Douglas & Michaels, 2004), and therefore they are more likely targets for programing focused on surveilling and educating parents (Collins, 2009; Elliott et al., 2015; LaBorde, 2009).

Child-Centered Parenting

None of the items from the IPAQ loaded together for the child-centered scale. Child-centered items from the IPAQ were largely indicated by beliefs that parents should make personal sacrifices by putting children's schedules before their own and beliefs that parenting should be adapted to fit individual children's needs (Liss et al., 2013). Child-centered beliefs may not be realistic for mothers who have to deal with multiple life challenges or who must prioritize their requirements of state supervision over parenting. It may be that mothers on supervision are unable to enact child-centered parenting methods or that they perceive such efforts to be ineffective based on other problematic circumstances such as children's antisocial behavior. The need to prioritize probation and parole requirements over parenting or to work long hours to support children may result in different expressions of child-centered parenting (Giordano, 2010; Robison & Hughes Miller, 2016). Thus, child-centered activities of justice-involved mothers may differ from the norms reflected by "experts" and middle-class women that are measured by the IPAQ. The limited fit of these items appears to validate previous studies on low-income, single, and justice-involved mothers indicating that they must negotiate parenting and other conflicting obligations related to their marginalization and involvement in the justice system (Brown & Bloom, 2009; Ferraro & Moe, 2003; Granja et al., 2015; Opsal, 2009; Robison & Hughes Miller, 2016). Child-centered beliefs of justice-involved mothers may be better evaluated by sacrifices such as isolating themselves from people who might provide social support due to their network members potential to negatively influence or harm their children (Cobbina et al., 2014), concealing their own struggles with issues such as addiction due to fear of custody loss (Hagan & Dinovitzer, 1999; Robison & Hughes Miller, 2016), and even accepting custody loss for the sake of their children's wellbeing (Brown & Bloom, 2009; Michalsen, 2011; Opsal, 2009, 2015; Robison & Hughes Miller, 2016).

Fulfillment

The results suggest that different questions may be required to measure beliefs regarding parental fulfillment for justice-involved mothers. Two of the items from the IPAQ concentrated on fulfillment experienced when children are infants. In comparison to the qualitative sample of mothers of 2–4 year old children that served as the basis for the IPAQ (Hays, 1996), participants in the current study were included if they had children who were 17 or younger while they were on community supervision. Questions could be added to assess beliefs about parental fulfillment for mothers rearing children in broader age groups such as items that tap into the joy parents experience while witnessing children develop. The weakness of this scale also may indicate that mothers on supervision don't feel as strongly as general populations do about the fulfillment that should be garnered from parenting due to the struggles that problematized their parenting such as criminal justice system involvement, financial hardships, addiction, child custody issues, multiple unplanned pregnancies, and children's behavioral problems (Arditti & Few, 2008; Brown & Bloom, 2009; Collins, 2009; Giordano, 2010; Robison & Hughes Miller, 2016). Justice-involved women's overwhelming experiences as single mothers may also thwart feelings of fulfillment in the parental role due to their exhausting parenting responsibilities or their roles as children's sole providers which often requires them to work long hours away from their children. Items asking about women's gratification from providing for children and from spending leisure time with children may better gauge justice-involved mother's beliefs about the fulfillment from parenting.

Intensive Parenting Beliefs and Justice-Involved Mothers' Risks for Recidivism

Correlations among the two dimensions of intensive parenting identified for justice-involved women were examined to address the third research question, "Do these dimensions of intensive parenting relate to risks for recidivism for justice-involved mothers?" The results indicate that, like the original study, essentialism and all-consuming were significantly associated with lower levels of psychological wellbeing, which are risks for recidivism for justice-involved women. Specifically, in the current study both essentialism and the belief that parenting should be all-consuming were related to justice-involved mothers' higher levels of parenting stress and lower levels of self-efficacy. Justice-involved mothers with stronger beliefs that parenting should be all-consuming also exhibited higher levels of depression and anxiety as well as anger and hostility.

The findings from the correlations examined in this study are consistent with the consequences described in qualitative research on intensive parenting (Hays, 1996; Newman & Henderson, 2014; Wall, 2010), and the findings by the developers of the IPAQ (Liss et al., 2013; Rizzo et al., 2013). Specifically, the developers found associations of beliefs in the dimensions of essentialism and all-consuming related to women's frustration with the maternal role (Liss et al., 2013) and their greater struggles with mental health problems (Rizzo et al., 2013). This study substantiates that justice-involved women with these beliefs also experience heightened mental health problems which can put them at risk for continued offending. These findings and those from other research (Hays, 1996; Newman & Henderson, 2014; Wall, 2010) suggest that studying intensive parenting beliefs can help uncover how gendered norms manifest into problems for women. In this context, women with stronger intensive parenting beliefs regarding the gendered and consuming nature of parenting may exhibit higher risks for recidivism due to living with goals that conflict with the resources available to them and the level of contact they have with their children (Arditti & Few, 2008; Brown & Bloom, 2009; Robison & Hughes Miller, 2016). These conflicts may make the idealistic goals they develop as mothers less pragmatic and more troubling (Ferraro & Moe, 2003; Hagan & Dinovitzer, 1999). Justice-involved mothers with these beliefs also may experience guilt for their perception of failure in the past or for failure to reach goals to improve for children. Equally problematic, these beliefs may result in or be promoted by challenges faced by women that contributed to their trouble with the law and that place them at increased risk for recidivism, such as experiencing stress from child-rearing (Arditti & Few, 2008; Brown & Bloom, 2009; Garcia, 2016). The current study's support for the relation between intensive parenting beliefs and negative life circumstances demonstrates the importance of addressing gendered norms within institutions and popular rhetoric (Douglas & Michaels, 2004; Hays, 1996). It is critical to question widely undisputed value systems like intensive parenting that are considered common sense solutions to societal problems, but that reinforce the subordination of women and other marginalized social groups (Granja et al., 2015; Hays, 1996, Ferraro & Moe, 2003).

Practical Implications

Increasing awareness of the consequences and the struggles of mothers attempting to uphold intensive parenting expectations in this study and in previous research could help guide policies that are more compatible with gender equality. For instance, findings about intensive parenting suggest the need for legislation supporting both maternal and paternal leave by employers, and the provision of low-cost childcare and other supports for those struggling to work and care for children (Hays, 1996). Such assistance would provide needed investment into parent's and children's futures and would be far more effective in addressing societal problems than current practices that largely leave families with limited resources to their own devices (Douglas & Michaels, 2004).

The results in the current study suggest that women's risks for recidivism should be considered in tandem with their subscription to gendered norms such as intensive parenting beliefs. Since women's belief in essentialism, women's unique parental qualification, relates to several risks, the implementation of women-specific treatment should be carefully considered. These findings along with evidence that those who work with and evaluate justice-involved mothers commonly embrace traditional gendered values (Pollack, 2010; Schur, 1983; Willison & O'Brien, 2017), serve as possible explanations for findings that programs meant to assist justice-involved women can actually be counterproductive and harmful (Bertand, 1999; Erez, 1989; Morash, 2010). Interactions with justice-involved mothers on supervision and in parenting programs should be sensitive to women's specific needs as parents and as individuals. Practitioners should also recognize how their personal intensive parenting values and how programing that is guided by traditional gendered norms can act as obstacles to women addressing their personal needs and for gaining strengths in prosocial avenues outside of motherhood (Brown & Bloom, 2009). Taken together, the findings from this study and prior research indicate that women-specific programing should be rigorously evaluated to avoid the encouragement or reinforcement of gendered and essentialist expectations that may trigger or bolster women's risks for recidivism (Bertand, 1999; Bloom et al., 2004; Erez, 1989; Morash, 2010).

Also, correctional programs that commonly emphasize autonomy and motivations in guiding practice should consider the extent that such programs provide realistic standards for justice-involved populations (Brown & Bloom, 2009; Granja et al., 2015). Assuming autonomy and personal responsibility is often contradictory to the array of external circumstances that impact women's abilities to parent and desist from crime and substance use (Blakey, 2010; Brown & Bloom, 2009; Ferraro & Moe, 2003; Granja et al., 2015; Robison & Hughes Miller, 2016). Implying that motivations and individual responsibility are the primary ways to rectify personal and parental challenges ignores circumstantial and systemic barriers to change. Those interacting with justice-involved mothers should consider how traditional rhetoric and the emphasis on individual responsibility of mothers can produce cultural isolation, and prompt increased guilt and mothers' development of idealistic parenting goals that can contribute to problematic outcomes (Brown & Bloom, 2009; Ferraro & Moe, 2003).

Relatedly, the findings from this study suggest women's potentially problematic beliefs that parenting should be difficult and require great time and effort should be addressed through practice with justice-involved mothers. This conclusion is consistent with research in the field of criminal justice that highlights the consequences of intensive parenting expectations and the need for programs to use resources to help struggling mothers meet their personal and familial needs, rather than focusing on women's performance of ideal parenting (Brown & Bloom, 2009; Ferraro & Moe, 2003; Granja et al., 2015; Opsal, 2009). A careful evaluation of the effectiveness and the realistic nature of programing and "expert" advice provided to justice-involved mothers is necessary to identify program features that could lead to or alleviate their parenting challenges. Those that interact with justice-involved mothers could identify parenting programs and sources of assistance that offer women information on strategies for managing parenting in ways that emphasize the importance of meeting their personal needs. Like combating problematic essentialist beliefs, the findings from this study suggest that practitioners could assist mothers that believe parenting should consume their time and energy by encouraging them to seek assistance from other sources of prosocial support. This may include assisting mothers in establishing connections with new prosocial support systems, and in mending relationships with prosocial family members who could provide mothers with needed emotional and instrumental support in parenting. Similar to the conclusions made by other scholars considering traditional gender norms and intensive parenting (Brown & Bloom, 2009; Hays, 1996; Jarrett, 1999; Pollack, 2004; Willison & O'Brien, 2017), this study indicates that mothers struggling with time-consuming parenting responsibilities and parenting stress should be equipped with information and tools that make parenting less challenging. Resources focused on managing parenting stress and behavioral problems of children could enable mothers to employ parenting strategies that are less strenuous (Hays, 1996; Jarrett, 1999). Also, the provision of wraparound requirements and services could reduce the burden of the extensive requirements of supervision for those who must spend time on child-rearing and on requirements for CPS (Pollack, 2004; Willison & O'Brien, 2017).

Limitations and Directions for Future Research

Though the current study offers insight on the potential consequences of justice-involved mother's subscription to intensive parenting beliefs, there are several limitations to this research. First, this was a preliminary correlational examination on the intensive parenting beliefs and risks for recidivism among justice-involved mothers. A complex regression involving multiple variables, as well as a structural model specifying the directionality of relationships among these variables should be conducted in the future. The findings from this study could direct more complex models as there is now evidence of the statistical associations between particular dimensions of intensive parenting and justice-involved mothers' specific risks for recidivism. Also, a replication of this study should be conducted with another large sample to validate and improve the dimensions intensive parenting captured in the current study of justice-involved mothers using the IPAQ. Based on this research, additional items should incorporate beliefs regarding father's caregiving abilities and responsibilities, the importance of expending financial resources in child-rearing, the value of seeking out and adhering to expert advice on parenting, the importance of protecting children and making sacrifices for children that are common for justice-involved mothers, and also the significance of fulfillment for parents throughout child development.

Although this study examines how intensive parenting beliefs manifest and relate to risks for a more racially diverse population than the original study, a serious limitation of this work is that it does not consider how intensive parenting beliefs differ for individuals at different intersections of society. Since intensive parenting is rooted in White, middle class society, the inconsistencies in the IPAQ results for the justice-involved mothers may support findings from qualitative research indicating that intensive parenting may not be valued as highly or may be performed differently by mothers of color and mothers who have fewer resources and limited contact with their children (Collins, 2009; Granja et al., 2015; Jarrett, 1999; Robison & Hughes Miller, 2016). Since the focus of this initial study was on the application of the IPAQ and the potential consequences of intensive parenting beliefs for justice-involved mothers, a more complex analysis including these sociodemographic variables is beyond the scope of this study. A next step in this research is to examine more complex models that include such sociodemographic indicators as well as indicators of women's pathways to crime such as their histories of trauma and mental illness. Understanding how expectations and beliefs concerning intensive parenting differ for those at various intersections of society would extend knowledge about how such beliefs relate to negative outcomes for justice-involved individuals with different backgrounds and life experiences. An examination of the relationship between women's intensive parenting beliefs and their pathways to crime could also clarify how women's experiences of adversity such as trauma, single parenthood, and economic marginalization shape or are shaped by their intensive parenting beliefs.

Another limitation of this study is that it was cross-sectional and took place several years after the participants started supervision, prohibiting the examination of the temporal ordering of mothers' beliefs and risks for recidivism. Intensive parenting beliefs should be measured when women are sentenced to supervision and then at intervals following experiences on supervision to better account for the ways in which interactions within the criminal justice system may impact beliefs as well as to establish time order on the impact of such beliefs on risks and recidivism. It would also be interesting to incorporate measures of guilt and shame, and parental goal discrepancy since research has indicated that these feelings are the result of intensive parenting beliefs and can produce negative outcomes for women (Brown & Bloom, 2009; Ferraro & Moe, 2003; Henderson et al., 2016). Additionally, it would be enlightening to examine how justice-involved women are held to intensive parenting expectations, and how their beliefs developed. Understanding these circumstances could provide more insight into how women develop more problematic intensive parenting beliefs such as essentialism and all-consuming beliefs. Relatedly, researchers should ask women how long they've held their intensive parenting beliefs, as this would allow for more information on the impacts of supervision and programing on women's development of their beliefs. Though the current study has information on whether women attended parenting programs, information on the content of these programs, and the extent that such programs impacted women's intensive parenting beliefs is unknown. Knowledge on how justice-involved mothers' beliefs change with exposure to programs that employ different types of parenting rhetoric would allow for improved understanding of potentially harmful parenting programs attended by justice-involved women. Understanding these features would better inform the ways in which criminal justice practitioners and others working with justice-involved women could asses and alter practices to reduce the promulgation of harmful intensive parenting beliefs.

Funding

This work was supported by the National Science Foundation Grant No. 1430372 entitled The Effects of Identity Development on Women's Recidivism.

REFERENCES

Adams, E. A., Morash, M., Smith, S. W., & Cobbina, J. E. (2017). Women's experiences of motherhood, violations of supervision requirements and arrests. *British Journal of Criminology*, *57*, 1420–1441. https://doi.org/10.1093/bjc/azw092

Arditti, J., & Few, A. (2008). Maternal distress and women's reentry into family and community life. *Family Process*, *47*(3), 303–321. https://doi.org/10.1177/089124399013003005

Baker, P. L., & Carson, A. (1999). "I take care of my kids": Mothering practices of substance- abusing women. *Gender & Society*, *13*(3), 347–363. https://doi.org/10.1111/j.1545-5300.2008.00255.x

Baunach, P. J. (1985). *Mothers in prison*. Transaction Books.

Beavers, A. S., Lounsbury, J. W., Richards, J. K., Huck, S. W., Skolits, G. J., & Esquivel, S. L. (2013). Practical considerations for using exploratory factor analysis in educational research. *Practical Assessment, Research & Evaluation*, *18*, 1–13.

Belknap, J. (2014). *The invisible woman* (4th ed.). Cengage Learning.

Belknap, J., & Holsinger, K. (2006). The gendered nature of risk factors for delinquency. *Feminist Criminology*, *1*(1), 48–47. https://doi.org/10.1177/1557085105282897

Bertand, M. (1999). Incarceration as a gendering strategy. *Canadian Journal of Law and Society*, *14*, 45–60. https://doi.org/10.1017/S0829320100005925

Bentler, P. M. (1995). *EQS structural equations program manual*. Multivariate Software.

Blakey, J. M. (2010). *Struggle for custody: The salience of trauma among African American women navigating substance abuse treatment and child protection* [Doctoral dissertation]. Proquest. (3419611).

Bloom, B., Owen, B., & Covington, S. S. (2004). Women offenders and gendered effects of public policy. *Review of Policy Research*, *21*(1), 31–48. https://doi.org/10.1111/j.1541-1338.2004.00056.x

Bloom, B., Owen, B., Covington, S. S., & Raeder, M. S. (2003). *Gender-responsive strategies: research, practice, and guiding principles for women offenders* (pp. 133). National Institute of Corrections.

Brown, J. D. (2009). Choosing the right type of rotation in PCA and EFA. *JALT Testing & Evaluation SIG Newsletter*, *13*, 20–25.

Brown, M., & Bloom, B. (2009). Reentry and renegotiating motherhood: Maternal identity and success on parole. *Crime & Delinquency*, *55*, 313–336. https://doi.org/10.1177/0011128708330627

Bureau of Justice Statistics. (1997). *Correctional populations in the United States, 1995*. U.S. Department of Justice.

Cobbina, J. E., Morash, M., Kashy, D. A., & Smith, S. W. (2014). Race, neighborhood danger, and coping strategies among female probationers and parolees. *Race and Justice*, *4*(1), 3–28.

Collins, P. H. (2009). *Black feminist thought: Knowledge, consciousness and the politics of empowerment*. Routledge Classics https://doi.org/10.1177/2153368713517397

Costello, A. B., & Osborne, J. W. (2005). Best practices in exploratory factor analysis: Four recommendations for getting the most from your analysis. *Practical Assessment, Research & Evaluation*, *10*, 1–9. https://doi.org/10.4135/9781412995627.d8

Creswell, J. W., & Plano Clark, V. L. (2011). *Designing and conducting mixed methods research* (2nd ed.). Sage Publications, Inc.

Cronbach, L. J. (1951). Coefficient alpha and the internal structure of tests. *Psychometrika*, *16*(3), 297–334. https://doi.org/10.1007/BF02310555

Daly, K., & Chesney-Lind, M. (1988). Feminism and criminology. *Justice Quarterly*, *5*(4), 497–535. https://doi.org/10.1080/07418828800089871

Damaske, S. (2013). Work, family, and accounts of mothers' lives using discourse to navigate intensive mothering ideals. *Sociology Compass*, *7*(6), 436–444. https://doi.org/10.1111/soc4.12043

DeVellis, R. F. (1991). *Scale development*. Sage Publications.

Diener, R., Emmons, R. A., Larsen, R. J., & Griffin, S. (1985). The satisfaction with life scale. *Journal of Personality Assessment*, *49*(1), 71–75. https://doi.org/10.1207/s15327752jpa4901_13

Douglas, S. J., & Michaels, M. W. (2004). *The idealization of motherhood and how it has undermined all women: The mommy myth*. Free Press.

Elliott, S., Powell, R., & Brenton, J. (2015). Being a good mom: Low-income, black, single mothers negotiate intensive mothering. *Journal of Family Issues*, *36*(3), 351–370. https://doi.org/10.1177/0192513X13490279

Erez, E. (1989). Gender, rehabilitation, and probation decisions. *Criminology*, *27*(2), 307–327.

Fedock, G., Fries, L., & Kubiak, S. P. (2013). Service needs for incarcerated adults: Exploring gender differences. *Journal of Offender Rehabilitation*, *52*(7), 493–508. https://doi.org/10.1080/10509674.2012.759171

Ferraro, K. J., & Moe, A. M. (2003). Mothering, crime, and incarceration. *Journal of Contemporary Ethnography*, *32*(1), 9–40. https://doi.org/10.1177/0891241602238937

Garcia, J. (2016). Understanding the lives of mothers after incarceration: Moving beyond socially constructed definitions of motherhood. *Sociology Compass*, *10*(1), 3–11. https://doi.org/10.1111/soc4.12337

George, D., & Mallery, M. (2010). *SPSS for windows step by step: A simple guide and reference, 17.0 update* (10th ed.). Pearson.

Giordano, P. C. (2010). *Legacies of crime: A follow-up of the children of highly delinquent girls and boys*. Cambridge University Press.

Glaze, L. E., & Maruschak, L. M. (2008). *Parents in prison and their minor children* (Special report). Bureau of Justice Statistics.

Golden, R. (2005). *War on the family: Mothers in prison and the families they leave behind*. Routledge.

Granja, R., da Cunha, M. I. P., & Machado, H. (2015). Mothering from prison and ideologies of intensive parenting: Enacting vulnerable resistance. *Journal of Family Issues, 36*(9), 1212–1232. https://doi.org/10.1177/0192513X14533541

Greene, S., Haney, C., & Hurtado, A. (2000). Cycles of pain: Risk factors in the lives of incarcerated mothers and their children. *The Prison Journal, 80*(1), 3–23. https://doi.org/10.1177/0032885500080001001

Greenfeld, L. A., & Snell, T. L. (1999). *Women offenders* (Bureau of Justice Statistics Special Report NCJ 175688). U.S. Department of Justice.

Grella, C. E., & Greenwell, L. (2006). Correlates of parental status and attitudes toward parenting among substance-abusing women offenders. *The Prison Journal, 86*(1), 89–113. https://doi.org/10.1177/0032885505283925

Hagan, J., & Dinovitzer, R. (1999). Collateral consequences of imprisonment for children, communities, and prisoners. In M. Tonry & J. Petersilia (Ed.), *Prisons* (pp. 121–162). Chicago, IL: University of Chicago Press. https://doi.org/10.1086/449296

Hays, S. (1996). *The cultural contradictions of motherhood.* New Haven, CT: Yale University Press.

Henderson, A., Harmon, S., & Newman, H. (2016). The price mothers pay, even when they are not buying it: Mental health consequences of idealized motherhood. *Sex Roles, 74*(11–12), 512–526. https://doi.org/10.1007/s11199-015-0534-5

Hu, L., & Bentler, P. M. (1995). Evaluation model fit. In R. H. Hoyle (Eds.), *Structural equation modeling: Concepts, issues, and applications* (pp. 76–99). Sage.

Jarrett, R. L. (1999). Successful parenting in high-risk neighborhoods. *The Future of Children, 9*(2), 45–50. https://doi.org/10.2307/1602704

Kaeble, D., & Bonczar, T. P. (2016). *Probation and parole in the United States, 2015.* Bureau of Justice Statistics.

Kaiser, H. F. (1958). The varimax criterion for analytic rotation in factor analysis. *Psychometrika, 23*(3), 187–200. https://doi.org/10.1007/BF02289233

Kessler, R. (1998). Sex differences in DSM-III-R psychiatric disorders in the United States: Results from the national comorbidity survey. *Journal of the American Medical Women Association, 53,* 142–155.

LaBorde, N. (2009). *Raising children the American way: Court-mandated parenting education in Almeda, California* [Doctoral dissertation]. Proquest, Ann Arbor, Michigan.

Langan, N. P., & Pelissier, B. M. (2001). Gender differences among prisoners in drug treatment. *Journal of Substance Abuse, 13*(3), 291–301. https://doi.org/10.1016/S0899-3289(01)00083-9

Laudet, A. B. (2011). The case for considering quality of life in addiction research and clinical practice. *Addiction Science & Clinical Practice, 6*(1), 44–55.

Laudet, A. B., Becker, J. B., & White, W. L. (2009). Don't wanna go through that madness no more: Quality of life satisfaction as predictor of sustained remission from illict drug misuse. *Substance Use & Misuse, 44,* 227–252. https://doi.org/10.1080/10826080802714462

Liss, M., Schiffrin, H. H., Mackintosh, V. H., Mile-McLean, H., & Erchull, M. J. (2013). Development and validation of a quantitative measure of intensive parenting attitudes. *Journal of Child and Family Studies, 22*(5), 621–636. https://doi.org/10.1007/s10826-012-9616-y

Lynch, S. M., Dehart, D. D., Belknap, J. E., Green, B. L., Dass-Brailsford, P., Johnson, K. A., & Whalley, E. (2014). A multisite study of the prevalence of serious mental illness, PTSD, and substance use disorders of women in jail. *Psychiatric Services, 65*(5), 670–674. https://doi.org/10.1176/appi.ps.201300172

Mallik-Kane, K., & Visher, C. A. (2008). *Health and prisoner reentry: How physical, mental, and substance abuse conditions shape the process of reintegration.* Urban Institute.

Mauer, M., Potler, C., & Wolf, R. (1999). *Gender and justice: Women, drugs, and sentencing policy.* The Sentencing Project.

McLoyd, V. C. (1990). The impact of economic hardship on Black families and children: Psychological distress, parenting, and socioemotional development. *Child Development, 61*(2), 311–346. https://doi.org/10.1111/j.1467-8624.1990.tb02781.x

Michalsen, V. (2011). Mothering as a life course transition: Do women go straight for their children. *Journal of Offender Rehabilitation, 50*(6), 349–366. https://doi.org/10.1080/10509674.2011.589887

Morash, M. (2010). *Women on probation and parole.* Northeastern University Press.

Muhammad, B. M. (2012). Exploring the silence among children of prisoners: A descriptive Study [Doctoral dissertation]. Proquest.

Muthén, L.K., & Muthén, B.O. (1998-2017). *Mplus User's Guide. Eighth Edition.* Los Angeles, CA: Muthén & Muthén. https://www.statmodel.com/download/usersguide/MplusUserGuideVer_8.pdf

Neff, J., & Waite, D. (2007). Male versus female substance abuse patterns among incarcerated juvenile offenders: Comparing strain and social learning variables. *Justice Quarterly, 24*(1), 106–132. https://doi.org/10.1080/07418820701201024

Newman, H. D., & Henderson, A. C. (2014). The modern mystique: Institutional mediation of hegemonic motherhood. *Sociological Inquiry, 84*(3), 472–491. https://doi.org/10.1111/soin.12037

Northcutt-Bohmert, M. (2016). The role of transportation disadvantage for women on community supervision. *Criminal Justice and Behavior*, *43*, 1522–1540. https://doi.org/10.1177/0093854816654267

O'Brien, P. (2001). "Just like baking a cake": Women describe the necessary ingredients for successful reentry after incarceration. *Families in Society*, *82*, 287–295. https://doi.org/10.1606/1044-3894 200

Office of National Drug Control Policy. (2013). *In-custody treatment and offender reentry.*

Opsal, T. (2009). Women on parole: Understanding the impact of surveillance. *Women & Criminal Justice*, *19*, 306–328. https://doi.org/10.1080/08974450903224345

Opsal, T. (2015). It's their world, so you've just got to get through": Women's experiences of parole governance. *Feminist Criminology*, *10*(2), 188–207. https://doi.org/10.1177/1557085114539723

Pavot, W., & Diener, E. (1993). Review of the satisfaction with life scale. *Psychological Assessment*, *5*(2), 164–172. https://doi.org/10.1007/978-90-481-2354-4_5

Payne, B. K., Gainey, R. R., & Carey, C. S. (2005). All in the family: Gender, family crimes, and later criminality. *Women & Criminal Justice*, *16*, 73–89. https://doi.org/10.1300/J012v16n04_04

Peters, R. H., Strozier, A. L., Murrin, M. R., & Kearns, W. D. (1997). Treatment of substance abusing jail inmates: Examination of gender differences. *Journal of Substance Abuse Treatment*, *14*(4), 339–349. https://doi.org/10.1016/S0740-5472(97)00003-2

Petersilia, J. (2003). *When prisoners come home: Parole and prisoner reentry.* Oxford University Press.

Pollack, S. (2004). Anti-oppressive social work practice with women in prison: Destructive reconstructions and alternative practices. *British Journal of Social Work*, *34*(5), 693–707. https://doi.org/10.1093/bjsw/bch085

Pollack, S. (2007). "I'm just not good in relationships": Victimization discourses and the gendered regulation of criminalized women. *Feminist Criminology*, *2*(2), 158–174. https://doi.org/10.1177/1557085106297521

Pollack, S. (2010). Victimisation and Governance: 'Gender-responsive' discourses and correctional practice. In R. Sheehan, G. McIvor, & C. Trotter (Eds.), *Working with female offenders in the community* (pp. 110–126). Willan. https://doi.org/10.4324/9780203832950

Raykov, T., & Marcoulides, G. A. (2006). *A first course in structural equation modeling* (2nd ed.). Erlbaum.

Richie, B. E. (2001). Challenges incarcerated women face as they return to their communities: Findings from life history interviews. *Crime & Delinquency*, *47*, 368–389. https://doi.org/10.1177/0011128701047003005

Rizzo, K. M., Schiffrin, H. H., & Liss, M. (2013). Insight into the parenthood paradox: Mental health outcomes of intensive mothering. *Journal of Child and Family Studies*, *22*(5), 614–620. https://doi.org/10.1007/s10826-012-9615-z

Robison, K. J., & Hughes Miller, M. (2016). Decentering motherhood: Reentry strategies for women on parole and probation. *Women & Criminal Justice*, *26*, 319–339. https://doi.org/10.1080/08974454.2016.1145617

Romagnoli, A., & Wall, G. (2012). 'I know I'm a good mom': Young, low-income mothers' experiences with risk perception, intensive parenting ideology and parenting education programmes. *Health, Risk, and Society*, *14*(3), 273–289. https://doi.org/10.1080/13698575.2012.662634

Salisbury, E., & Van Voorhis, P. (2009). Gendered pathways: A quantitative investigation of women probationers' paths to incarceration. *Criminal Justice and Behavior*, *36*(6), 541–566. https://doi.org/10.1177/0093854809334076

Schermelleh-Engel, K., Moosbrugger, H., & Müller, H. (2003). Evaluating the fit of structural equation models: Tests of significance and descriptive goodness of fit measures. *Methods in Psychological Research*, *8*, 23–74.

Schreiber, J. B., Nora, A., Stage, F. K., Barlow, E. A., & King, J. (2006). Reporting structural equation modeling and confirmatory factor analysis results: A review. *The Journal of Educational Research*, *99*(6), 323–337. https://doi.org/10.3200/JOER.99.6.323-338

Schur, E. M. (1983). *Labeling women deviant. Gender, stigma, and social control.* Temple University Press.

Schwarz, G. (1978). Estimating the dimension of a model. *The Annals of Statistics*, *6*(2), 461–464. https://doi.org/10.1214/aos/1176344136

Seng, M., & Lurigio, A. J. (2005). Probation officers' views on supervising women probationers. *Women & Criminal Justice*, *16*, 65–85. https://doi.org/10.1300/J012v16n01_03

Sherer, M., Maddux, J. E., Mercandante, B., Prentice-Dunn, S., Jacobs, B., & Rogers, R. W. (1982). The Self-Efficacy Scale: Construction and validation. *Psychological Reports*, *51*(2), 663–671. https://doi.org/10.2466/pr0.1982.51.2.663

Tabachnick, B., & Fidell, L. (2001). *Using multivariate statistics.* Allyn & Bacon

The Sentencing Project. (2012). *Incarcerated women.* http://www.sentencingproject.org/doc/publications/cc_Incarcerated_Women_Factsheet_Dec2012final.pdf

Uggen, C., & Kruttschnitt, C. (1998). Crime in the breaking: Gender differences in desistance. *Law & Society Review*, *32*, 339–366. https://doi.org/10.2307/827766

Van Voorhis, P. (2012). On behalf of women offenders: Women's place in the science of evidence-based practice. *Criminology & Public Policy*, *11*(2), 111–145. https://doi.org/10.1111/j.1745-9133.2012.00793.x

Van Voorhis, P., Bauman, A., & Brushett, R. (2012). *Revalidation of the Women's Risk Needs Assessment: Pre-release results.* University of Cincinnati.

Van Voorhis, P., Bauman, A., & Brushett, R. (2013). *Revalidation of the Women's Risk Needs Assessment: Probation Results*. University of Cincinnati.

Van Voorhis, P., Wright, E. M., Salisbury, E., & Bauman, A. (2010). Women's risk factors and their contributions to existing risk/needs assessment: The current status of a gender- responsive supplement. *Criminal Justice and Behavior*, *37*(3), 261–288. https://doi.org/10.1177/0093854809357442

Vaske, J. J. (2008). *Survey research and analysis: Applications in parks, recreation and human dimensions*. Venture Publishing Inc.

Wall, G. (2010). Mothers' experiences with intensive parenting and brain development discourse. *Women's Studies International Forum*, *33*(3), 253–263.

West, C., & Zimmerman, D. H. (1987). Doing gender. *Gender & Society*, *1*, 125–151. https://doi.org/10.1177/0891243287001002002

Willison, J. S., & O'Brien, P. (2017). A feminist call for transforming the criminal justice system. *Affilia: Journal of Women and Social Work*, *32*(1), 37–49. https://doi.org/10.1177/0886109916658080

Managing Motherhood: How Incarcerated Mothers Negotiate Maternal Role-Identities with Their Children's Caregivers

Ebonie Cunningham Stringer

ABSTRACT

Women's incarceration rates have increased dramatically within the last 40 years. Many of the women who find themselves in the grips of confinement are mothers. Maternity can be central to women's identities, making them reluctant to relinquish mothering roles once they become incarcerated. When women serve time, they can no longer be directly responsible for day-to-day caregiving for their young children. Thus, children are often placed in the care of proxy caregivers. Notwithstanding, many women retain their maternal identities and wish to engage as mothers while they are incarcerated. As such, women must manage motherhood with and through their children's caregivers. Using group interviews, this study investigates how maternity is managed from prison with children's caregivers. Findings reveal the strategies women employ to maintain their role-identities as mothers while serving time. Policy implications are discussed.

INTRODUCTION

Motherhood can be a primary source of identity for women who have children. Through play, observation and interaction, girls often internalize social expectations that mothers be present and active as nurturers, emotionally supportive, and teachers to their children (Boyd, 1989; Bromberg, 1983; Grief, 1985). "Good" mothers are commended for their ability to provide direction, structure and discipline for their young. Historically, sociobiological explanations have presented mothering as the natural priority and inevitable destiny of women. Given this assumption, crime-involved women may be viewed as unfit, abhorrent, unnatural, violent and most dreadful among law violators, even when they commit nonviolent crimes (Baldwin, 2015; Lombroso et al., 1895; Merlo & Pollock, 2006). This belief persists despite the fact that many crime-involved women value their families and view motherhood as the most important part of their identity.

No mother is perfect, and imprisoned women are no exception (Boudin, 1998). The blueprint for conventional maternity lauds "intensive mothering," which requires mothers to selflessly expend a great deal of time, money and energy in rearing their children (Hays, 1996). Intensive mothers are expected to cope with the challenges of life with children without any difficulty or failure (Von Weller et al., 2018). However, "intensive mothering" may be an unrealistic, demoralizing, controlling and punishing standard for incarcerated women (Aiello, 2016; Aiello & McQueeney, 2019; Collins, 2000; Glenn et al., 1994). The celebration of this model also disparages the mothering practices of poor, working class and minority women (Aiello, 2016; Collins, 2000; Glenn et al., 1994), all of which are disproportionately represented among incarcerated women. Nonetheless, three quarters of these mothers were primary caretakers to their children prior to incarceration (Bloom & Brown, 2011; Glaze & Maruschak, 2010; McGowan & Blumenthal, 1978; Green et al., 2000). Given that mothering implicates both *who* one is and *what* one does, imprisonment can upend the maternal role and threaten one's identity. Confined women are at a clear disadvantage when attempting to meet the physical and emotional demands of mothering. A mother serving time is with few exceptions separated by space and time from her children. Consequently, children are often placed in the care of proxy caregivers: grandparents, fathers, relatives, friends, and as a last resort foster care, to assume the role of caretaking in the physical absence of a mother (Enos, 2001).

Prisons as total institutions can isolate residents with rituals that effectively, and somewhat intentionally, strip women of their former identities and roles (Goffman, 1961). At intake, the incarcerated are relieved of personal effects and given a new identity: a number. Relics of their former life and identity can only be reclaimed once their time has been served. But reclamation of the maternal role is not easily accomplished if some semblance of it is not maintained during a woman's incarceration (Freudenberg et al., 2008). Prison mail and visitation policies, as well as cost prohibitive phone calls, make it difficult for women to maintain contact with the outside world where their children often remain (Hairston, 2007; Margolies & Kraft-Stolar, 2006). Mothers can go weeks, months and even years without seeing their children or hearing their voices (Glaze & Maruschak, 2010). Some prisons feature parenting and child visitation programs, but these solutions are far from perfect. Under such deleterious conditions, we might expect women to feel powerless and abandon maternal identities (Baunach, 1985).

Though obstacles to motherhood in prison can seem insurmountable, they may not be for women who cling to maternal identities. Women can be motivated by their children to survive "the cage," desist from crime (Brown & Bloom, 2009) and be innovative in ways that allow them to remain mothers. Some women find institutional support and allies to motherhood among other residents, prison staff and with the help of gender responsive programing (Aiello, 2016; Morash et al., 1998). These support systems, when they exist, can help women to manage mothering within the prison structure. However, the persons who care for a woman's children during her incarceration can be critical (Poehlmann et al., 2008). They may determine the nature of women's interactions with their children, and ultimately whether and how mothers *do* mothering while incarcerated (Enos, 2001). This study investigates how imprisoned women manage mothering role-identities through relationships with their children's caregivers.

MOTHERING ROLES AND IDENTITY: A THEORETICAL FRAMEWORK

Gendered role performance is often dictated by cultural expectations of behavior that are internalized through socialization processes that initiate in early childhood (Mangus, 1957). Roles such as that of a mother are usually learned through observation and imitation of significant others and can shape role performance in ways that tend to reflect social expectations (Biddle, 1986; Morgan & Schwalbe, 1990; Turner, 1991). Social roles are inclusive of what people do and ideas about what people *should* do when occupying particular social positions (Morgan & Schwalbe, 1990; Von Weller et al., 2018). However, whether by choice or circumstance, social actors do not always embody prescribed role expectations. Yet, once internalized and inhabited, roles can become central to a person's identity (Mangus, 1957). Thus, mothering, as a role-identity, is indicative of both identity and behavior (Von Weller et al., 2018). Yet a woman's perceptions about her ability to perform the maternal role in a socially acceptable way can shape her view of herself as a mother.

The management of role-identities can be a complex process in which people attempt to understand and negotiate who they are and how they fit into the scheme of things. The complexity of this process is exacerbated when an individual's social position changes unexpectedly or in a way that does not compliment role expectations. Such is the case when a mother goes to prison.

The successful (re)negotiation or eventual departure from a role-identity can be highly influenced by significant others. Indeed, the embodiment of any role-identity is shaped by interaction with significant others who can support or diminish the roles we play. Significant others are the persons whose care, opinions, affection and/or approval are especially desired (James, 1968; Kendall, 2012). As such, they are key to the development of the self and subsequent identity (Kendall, 2012).

Among incarcerated women, children's caregivers represent significant others whose opinions and approval matter. Caregivers' roles matter in terms of affection, a woman's ability to fulfill the mothering role and consequently the feelings women have about themselves as mothers. However, mothers are not passive consumers. When mothers perceive that their role-identities are viewed disparagingly, they may employ agency to engage in identity management. The notion of *agency* emphasizes the dynamic process by which individuals construct and claim their identities (McCall & Simmons, 1966; Stets & Burke, 2000). Depending on their social situation, people have varying degrees of freedom in devising for themselves the characters that comprise role-identity (Mangus, 1957; McCall & Simmons, 1966). While the power of human agency cannot be trivialized, the social structure's impact on human actors can far exceed an individual's impacts on the structure (Stryker, 1980). Prisons are the proverbial illustration of how a powerful social structure can diminish individual agency and shape the lives of its inhabitants.

The process of identity management often incorporates biographical narratives from social actors. These narratives can be used as tools to aid the individual in subverting deprecatory labels and negative self-feelings (Geiger & Fischer, 2003). These stories often retrospectively interpret life events to make sense of current conditions (Bruner, 1998). Likewise, narratives may minimize missteps, justify behavior or allow a person to take responsibility for their actions (Scott and Lyman, 1968), all while attempting to salvage or negotiate identity in the eyes of self and the social audience. Nonetheless, in the absence of role support, social actors may experience distress and difficulty in negotiating their roles (Burke, 1991; Stets & Burke, 2000).

In her study of imprisoned women, peer counselors, correctional officers, and prisons staff, Schram (1999) found that some women internalize and negatively react to criticism from staff about their mothering roles. This in turn can minimize mothers' attempts at role performance and endanger mother-child relationships. Schram's study offers evidence that mothers want to feel valued in their roles by people whose opinions and feelings they hold in high esteem. It can be assumed that when mothers choose their children's caregivers, they do so because among other things, they have some measure of respect or admiration for the persons they select. Thus, the degree to which women feel that their roles are valued and supported by caregivers as significant others may have important implications for whether and how they maintain their role-identities as mothers.

IMPRISONED MOTHERS

Policy agendas such as the war on drugs and truth in sentencing have dramatically increased the number of women in the criminal justice system (Crawford, 2003; Drug Policy Alliance, 2016; Sentencing Project, 2019). Are imprisoned women especially violent and dreadful as early criminologists theorized (Lombroso et al., 1895)? Are they unfit to mother? There is little empirical support for these ideas. Women comprise 8–10% of the prison population. Most are serving time for nonviolent offenses that are not necessarily related to child abuse, neglect or an inability to provide appropriate care for their children (Baldwin et al., 2015; Greenfield & Snell, 1999; Harrison & Beck, 2006; Snell & Morton, 1994). Women who are violent offenders are actually *less* likely to report being mothers (Glaze & Maruschak, 2010). A study of 104 mothers participating in a 15-week parenting program found that there was no significant difference in parenting behaviors between mothers who had been convicted of crimes and those who had not

(Thompson & Harm, 2000). Thus, most imprisoned mothers do not fit dreadful typecasts and may, in fact, share many similarities with non-incarcerated mothers.

Imprisoned mothers must contend with the reality that someone else is responsible for day-to-day care of their children. This can be especially difficult for women who embrace intensive mothering. Children's caregiving arrangements can have important implications for a woman's role as a mother in the long and short-term. For younger children, caregivers can make simple, but significant decisions such as whether mothers and children talk by phone or correspond by mail. They can also determine whether children visit their mothers or participate in family programs when available (Poehlmann et al., 2010). In the long-term, caregiving arrangements can determine whether mothers will have legal custody or access to their children once they are released from prison. For children placed in the custody of the state or foster care, the likelihood that parental rights will be terminated may be exacerbated (Iskikian, 2019; Raimon et al., 2009; Smith, 2006). Incarcerated parents with children in foster care who have not abused, neglected or endangered their children are more likely to lose parental rights than parents who have physically or sexually assaulted their children (Iskikian, 2019). Further, previous research indicates that women's incarceration experience and post-incarceration outlook has implications for the salience of a mother's identity (Stringer & Barnes, 2012). Given these factors, the mother-caregiver relationship may be key to understanding the nature of mother-child relationships and maternal identity among imprisoned women.

CAREGIVING ARRANGEMENTS FOR THE CHILDREN OF INCARCERATED MOTHERS

Incarceration separates an estimated 147,400 dependent aged children in America from their mothers (Glaze & Maruschak, 2010). Nearly 80% of these children are between 1 and 14 years of age (McGowan & Blumenthal, 1978; Morton & Williams, 1998; Sentencing Project, 2012). Incarcerated mothers most commonly identify grandmothers (45–50%) as their children's caregivers regardless of race or ethnicity (Glaze & Maruschak, 2010; Hill, 2003; Johnston, 1997; Philips & Gleeson, 2007; Sentencing Project, 2019). Following a mother's arrest, the number of children living in their father's care doubles—at least temporarily. Between 25% and 37% of children end up living with their fathers while their mothers serve time (Philips & Gleeson, 2007; Sentencing Project, 2012). Many of these fathers previously lived apart from their children. Though children may be placed in their father's care, it is not always clear who is responsible for the day-to-day care of children. According to Glaze and Maruschak (2010), fathers living with their young children often rely on others to provide daily care for them. Twenty-three percent (23%) of mothers report that their children are living with other relatives such as aunts or older siblings (Glaze & Maruschak, 2010; Sentencing Project, 2012). Not surprisingly, children living with kin report feeling greater love and safety than those living in foster care (Hairston, 1999). Incarcerated women who formed early positive attachments to their own mothers have more positive co-parenting experiences when children are placed with the mothers who raised them. This co-parenting relationship is marked by mutual support and more frequent contact with children (Loper & Clarke, 2013). As such, grandparents and other relative caregivers are often preferred by imprisoned mothers (Enos, 2001).

Though kinship care is often preferred, it may not be without its challenges. Caregivers often struggle to foster relationships between children and their incarcerated parents (Margolies & Kraft-Stolar, 2006). Caregivers may also feel shame, anger, stress and financial strain when a mother goes to prison (Johnston, 1997; Travis & Solomon, 2003). A mother's incarceration can constitute an adverse childhood experience with cumulative effects, including children feeling conflicted between their mother and caregivers, emotional disturbances, damaged self-esteem, an increased risk for childhood delinquency and future imprisonment (Bloom & Steinhart, 1993; Greenburg, 2006; Henriques, 1982; Johnston, 1997; McGowan & Blumenthal, 1978; Morton &

Williams, 1998; Poehlmann, 2005b; Turney, 2018). According to Poehlmann (2005a, 2005b), knowing that their children have stability, emotional and behavioral support is helpful for a mother who is coping with incarceration.

INCARCERATED MOTHERS' RELATIONSHIPS WITH CAREGIVERS

A lack of daily involvement with their children is cited as one of the most challenging aspects of incarceration among women (Ingram-Fogel, 1993). Poehlmann (2005a) found that when mothers and caregivers have relationships marked by conflict, there is less visitation and phone contact with children. However, when mothers and caregivers agree upon their roles, their relationships fare better and children are more likely to experience continuity in care, rather than being moved between households (Johnston, 1997). Thus, the relationship between mothers and their children's caregivers can have implications for children's well-being as well as a woman's relationship with her children (Poehlmann, 2005a; Poehlmann et al., 2008). Yet few studies investigate the practical strategies that women use to manage motherhood in concert with their children's caregivers. This is the primary task undertaken in the present study. Using group interview data from incarcerated mothers, the ways in which mother-caregiver relationships impact the mothering role-identity are explored.

Mothering among incarcerated women cannot be romanticized. Often, the aggregate effects of women's abuse, addiction, poverty and trauma can inhibit or attenuate mothering role-identities even before incarceration. Not all incarcerated mothers are committed to motherhood and some may relinquish these roles if they are unable to reconcile caregiver relationships, past behavior or their present contexts with mothering. While caregivers and the prison structure itself can erect barriers to performing maternal roles, this study is an investigation of the ways in which women, with varying degrees of success, attempt to manage these roles and maintain their identities as mothers. Group interviews with imprisoned women are used as a means of drawing out mothers' biographical sketches and motherhood narratives (Geiger & Fischer, 2003) in order to better understand how they manage the maternal role-identity.

METHODS

Research Site

With the approval of the University's Institutional Review Board and the state's Department of Correction, a three-part study was conducted at a Midwest women's prison. The components of the study include a survey of the entire prison population, group interviews with mothers and participant observation in the prison's parenting program. The present study draws upon data collected during group interviews with mothers. While complete demographic data is not available for group interview participants, findings from the survey administered to the entire prison population show that nearly 73% of the residents have biological, adopted and/or foster children. Sixty-three percent (63%) report living with their children prior to incarceration. These findings align with existing research suggesting that many imprisoned women are mothers and are significantly involved in their children's daily lives prior to incarceration (Glaze & Maruschak, 2010).

Sample and Procedures

This study is based on group interviews with a purposive convenience sample. Group interviews are used in order to give women voice and gain first-hand, in depth knowledge of women's maternal experiences. Women were primarily recruited through flyers posted in housing units and announcements made by the researcher during the survey administration. Group interviews

Table 1. Age for prison population.

Age	
Mean	42 years
Mode	21 years
Median	34 years
Range	16–79 years

Total population $N = 288$.

Table 2. Marital status of prison population.

Marital status	%	*N*
Single/Never Married	44	127
Single/Cohabitating	10	30
Married	11	32
Separated	8	23
Divorced	17	50
Widowed	7	20
Mothers in population	73	210

Total population $N = 288$.

Table 3. Offense categories of the prison population.

Offense categories	%	*N*
Drug offenses	20	58
Violent offenses	44	126
Sex offenses	5	15
Property offenses	15	43
Economic offenses	9	35
Other	5	15
Recidivists	26	76
Serving time for multiple offenses	38	108

Total population $N = 288$.

were conducted in prison classrooms. No guards or prison staff were present. Each mother was asked to select a pseudonym as not to be identified in transcripts or future publications. Participants were compensated with a child's stationary kit which included colored paper and stickers for writing letters to children. All participants were advised of the voluntary nature of group interviews and gave their written consent to participate.

Two women moderators conducted nine, one-hour group interviews with approximately 55 women. The number of participants in each group varied between five to ten women. The sample is comprised of women who are mothers, grandmothers and great grandmothers. One aunt who co-parented with her siblings prior to her incarceration is also included in the sample. About 49% ($n = 27$) are identified as White, and 23% ($n = 13$) are identified as African American. Three percent (3%) of the sample is identified as multiracial and 3% are identified as Hispanic ($n = 4$). Twenty percent (20%) ($n = 11$) of respondent's races could not be identified. On average, respondents have 2.9 children (biological, adopted and/or foster). At the time of data collection, women had served between 2 months and 24 years on their current sentence, though women were not asked to report the length of their sentences. Neither were participants asked directly about their marital status, age or crimes. However, demographic data was collected in the survey administered to the entire prison population from which the sample is drawn. These data are presented in Tables 1–3.

Data Analysis

Moderators used an open-ended discussion guide for all group interviews. This format allows respondents to build narratives and discourse around the issues and experiences most important to them. As such, mothers have the opportunity to tell their own stories, from their perspective, on their own terms (Gubrium & Holstein, 1997). Such narratives can be key to the management of role identities (Bruner, 1998; Geiger & Fischer, 2003). The open-ended guide also allows the moderator to clarify respondents' intentions, beliefs, and attitudes, while allowing for inter-group comparisons (Kerlinger, 1964).

Group interviews were audio-taped, transcribed and analyzed using content analysis. Data analysis is initially based on pre-coded themes contrived from the research questions and the literature. However, new themes emerge during analysis. In coding and analysis, the researcher breaks down the narratives generated in group interviews and arranges them in ways that allow for the creation of new categories and their relationships to one another (Maxwell, 2009). During the process, the researcher moves back and forth between conceptualization, analysis and interpretation (Altheide, 2004), being careful to center the language respondents use and the meaning conveyed through words and affect. Special consideration is given to the experiences and topics that respondents emphasize as important. Finally, the researcher is sensitive to the ways in which the meaning of specific experiences and motherhood in general is constructed within the context of the group (Bryman, 2004). Findings along with representative quotes from respondents are presented below.

FINDINGS

Caregiving Arrangements

Sample mothers agreed that surrendering the care of their children to other individuals was often a painful transition. Lexus, a White mother of two sons states:

> [I'm] going through all this therapy and self-help groups to feel better, to not have low self-esteem, to become a healthier person. Yet I feel inadequate in the fact that someone else is taking care of my child.

Other women shared this view. Christa is an African American mother of three girls. She delivered her youngest daughter while incarcerated, only six weeks prior to our meeting. She relays,

> ... (crying) I'll be ok. This is going to be one of my harder times .... Because ... I love my kids. My kids are with me all the time. I didn't plan on being incarcerated so my mom could raise my kids cause that's not her job, it was mine.

It is clear from these representative quotes that sample women have internalized conventional expectations that mothers be present and accounted for in the daily lives of their children. While separation from their children is a stark reality that shapes their maternal experiences, so too do children's specific living arrangements.

Mothers were asked to speak about their children's living arrangements since their incarceration. A range of surrogate caregivers are represented among respondents. Given cultural expectations about women as caretakers, it is not surprising that women most often assume caregiving for respondents' children. Eighty-two percent (82%) of respondents reported that at least one of their children's caregivers was another woman. Maternal grandmothers, followed by other persons with whom mothers have a familial relationship, are the most frequently reported caregivers. However, the number of fathers who took on caregiving responsibilities is not insignificant. Thirty-three percent (33%) of respondents said that children's fathers assumed caregiving for at least one of their children. While relative caretakers are most common, a small proportion of mothers report that their children are in non-familial caregiving arrangements with friends, foster or adoptive parents. Mothers' comments suggest that this option is employed when family members are unwilling or unable to take on the responsibility of caregiving. Helen, a White mother of five children, spoke about her only dependent-aged child: "He's in a foster home right now ... I just had that done ... cause I didn't have nobody. My mother, she's dead ... I didn't have nobody else."

In some families, caregiving responsibilities are delegated among multiple persons. Mothers are more commonly report multiple caregivers in families with multiple children or multiple fathers. Women also report unique challenges associated with multiple caregivers. Lexus sadly shares her experiences with her sons:

> They're separated. They see each other at their visits here every other week and sometimes their dad's will get together maybe once a month and let them spend the night. But up until almost 3 years ago when I got arrested, they had never lived outside of one another ... So not only are they dealing with the separation of me being incarcerated, they're dealing with the separation of being apart from one another.

Justina is a White mother of three children. Each child has a different caregiving arrangement in three different cities. She states:

> I'm in my fourth year ... I haven't seen all of my children at one time except for [once] since I've been down ... and they don't get to see each other ... very often. All of my children aren't by the same father ... My mom had to take my son, or my son was going to end up in foster care, because I had my son here ... Of course she loves him, but she got sick. That's why he's with a friend of the family. Nobody ... let[s] my kids see their siblings ... so it's kind of hard.

Like Justina, many incarcerated mothers may feel challenged by their children's caregiving arrangements, especially when their children are living in separate households. Women's narratives suggest that the separation of their children into separate households creates difficulty in maintaining both maternal and sibling relationships. The maintenance of the maternal role is also complicated by variations in the perceived quality of care their children receive. When children are divided across different households, mothers must manage their roles with multiple persons, and disperse their emotional energy and resources across multiple households and caregivers. It can become increasingly difficult to remain bonded and active in the lives of all their children. Women can feel a double pang of guilt because incarceration has caused their children to lose both their mother and their siblings. Here, respondents illuminate an often-understated part of the mothering role: the pressure that mothers feel to keep their offspring relationally bonded to one another. As illustrated by Justina's comments, this becomes more difficult in multiple caregiver arrangements. However, when a mother chooses her children's caregiving arrangements, she may more easily manage her maternal role with and among caregivers.

The Power to Choose: Making Caregiver Arrangements for Children

Having some authority in choosing their children's caregiver seemed to ameliorate some of the challenges of separation and feelings of inadequacy. However, the degree of agency in choosing their children's caregivers varies among women. Mothers describe ideal caregiving arrangements as placements that keep children within the family. Interestingly, women's narratives reveal that "the family" was a term which almost exclusively referred to a mother's relatives rather than persons related to their children's fathers. In other words, keeping children within the mother's family was a priority. Maternal grandmothers were often preferred with other maternal relatives as a secondary choice. Women believe that these are persons with whom they share parenting ideals and whose decisions will often reflect their own wishes concerning children. A woman may also perceive that her relatives already share a meaningful relationship and care deeply for her children. Likewise, family members tend to have an affection for the incarcerated woman as a mother and as a person. As such these caregivers are perceived as being more open to supporting women as they manage mothering while incarcerated. This seems to set the stage for a woman's ability to effectively manage the maternal role-identity with caregivers. While speaking about her children's living arrangements, Beonka, an African American mother of two girls living with their maternal grandmother, says, "I wouldn't have it any other way... I want my children to stay within the family."

Notwithstanding women's preference for her relatives to care for children, women may admire fathers who willingly accept responsibility for their children. Despite the challenges of negotiating motherhood with two caregivers, Lexus says of her children's fathers, "They're good fathers... each one of their dads wanted them and they wanted that responsibility." When fathers have legal custody of their offspring, it is not always clear who is responsible for the day-to-day care of children. This mimics results found in other research (Glaze & Maruschak, 2010). It is clear from some respondents' narratives that mothers do not always acknowledge or know about women with whom fathers may have temporary or ongoing relationships or arrangements. These women may be responsible for providing or assisting in childcare. This truth was illuminated by Dee Dee, an African American mother who was expecting her third child at the time of data collection. She spoke about a recent phone conversation with her daughter:

> [My husband] has this mistress, whoever she might be. My daughter knows her as mother... but... [my daughter] ... knows I'm her mama and she tells me everything. And I think [my husband] does not like that because she's only three ... when I talked to her today, she was like, "Let me talk to my mama." And she got on the phone... She said, "We got pictures taken." I said, "Who?" "Me, and my daddy and my mama... "

That Dee Dee's child references her husband's mistress as mama suggests the possibility that the mistress may have a significant caregiving role for Dee Dee's daughter. Dee Dee's tone and subsequent verbiage indicate that this was a direct threat to her maternal identity. This case also illuminates that incarcerated mothers must manage motherhood with designated caregivers as well as other "mothers" in their children's lives. African American mothers in the sample are especially concerned about who their children know as "mama." They delineate the contexts in which this is acceptable, such as when children use the term to refer to maternal grandmothers and aunts. Ironically, Dee Dee encountered a second mistress in the prison who relayed that she too had been involved with Dee Dee's husband for a time, and that the child was often in her care. These circumstances, while far beyond the control of any incarcerated mother, can dramatically impact whether and how she manages her mothering role-identity. Dee Dee's case also demonstrates that while women may exercise agency to manage their children's living arrangements, they cannot negotiate the precise terms of that arrangement.

Some mothers are limited in their options or have no options at all as to what will happen with their children when they become incarcerated. Women whose children are not placed with relatives often express reluctance and resentment regarding the arrangement. V, an African American mother of three girls was expecting her fourth child, a baby girl, at the time of data collection. She shares her feelings of disappointment about her children having to live with a friend:

> So I'm down here with my children and all my family is up there. So basically all [my children] know is me. So by me being incarcerated, it makes it a lot harder on them than say if you had a cousin or auntie or something like that, a sister or whatever. I mean, you know, some close family that you can go to... So my children are with a friend of mine.

LaShaunna, an African American mother, also had little choice in her children's living arrangements. Her sister chose for her two daughters to live with another sister in Kentucky until they completed high school. Her sister then moved the girls to Florida to live with an uncle and attend college. LaShaunna, a professed Christian, supports her sister's choice because her children live in a religious environment that values education, as she does. However, she has not seen her children since her incarceration and rarely has phone contact with them or other relatives. LaShaunna's case is exemplary in that a lack of agency in arranging caregiving seems to coincide with a diminished ability to maintain contact or successfully manage an ongoing role in children's lives.

In some ways, LaShaunna is an anomaly. She presents as very supportive of those who raised and now support her children. However, among respondents, most women who do not choose their children's caregivers, do not support the living arrangements or the caregivers. For example, Nichole, an African American mother of three boys, does not support the decision that her brother and mother made to place two of her children with their father. Nichole views this as a poor choice that exposes her children to an inappropriate lifestyle and an environment with little structure. Nichole relays that the children's father makes no effort to facilitate or support her relationship with her children. Similarly, Janey, a White mother of six children, was disappointed when her children's living arrangement was altered by an overburdened caregiver, resulting in the separation of her three small children into two different households in two different states. Janey said of her informally adopted child with special needs,

> I knew when I took custody of [my son] that he would have problems learning … My sister … feels like she couldn't handle that with the other two [children] … [She says,] I'm not as strong as you. And so I don't agree about [her] sending [my son] to live in Kentucky with [my other sister] … See originally the three little ones were together. Then she said, Janey, I can't do that. I said, Well I don't agree. But I wouldn't want him any other place but with my other sister.

In her final analysis, what was most important to Janey is that her son stayed within "the family," or with maternal relatives. Though mothers like Janey may not be entirely satisfied with living arrangements, they may feel that it is best not to resist, lest they create tension between caregivers and themselves. If women like LaShaunna, V, and Janey can't *choose* their children's caregivers, the next best option is to *approve* of the arrangements that others have made. This was a part of an overarching strategy to *go along to get along* and remain in caregivers' good graces. To neither *choose* nor *approve* of children's caregivers seems to be an indication of a woman's limited agency and power to manage her maternal role-identity with caregivers. Conversely, the power to choose the person who cares for their children seems to predict the degree of agency women can employ to have access, an active role, or even authority in the lives of their children.

Having Authority as a Mother

In the study, mothers who exercise authority in their children's lives make decisions about children's caregiving, education, and/or extracurricular activities. For instance, Tammy, an African American mother of three, chose for her youngest daughter to live with her mother. Consequently, she has been able to act as a disciplinarian and decision maker in her daughter's life. In reference to her daughter, Tammy illustrates her parental authority:

> When she gets in trouble at school, I do have talks with her. She's not getting her work done in school, so now I'm letting her stay after school … [W]hen she was in the first grade, and the teachers was talking about … keeping her in the first grade … I told them yeah gone ahead and keep her back.

Likewise, Jaime a White mother, decided that her only child, an autistic daughter, would live with her parents. She recounts how she used her authority and influence as a mother to get her child the help she needs:

> My daughter was sexually molested, and she has a lot of issues with that … So, I had to start talking to my family again a couple months ago because I started noticing issues with her on her visits. I talked to my parents to get her back in therapy, which they've started her therapy again.

Toni, a White mother, made arrangements for her only child to live with his maternal grandmother, who allows her to exercise a great deal of authority in his life:

> I wrote Big Brothers Big Sisters and he's got a big sister right now that's my age and she does a lot of the same things I do. I wrote Boys and Girls Club so he's going there after school to do structured activities

and keep him … hopefully on the right path … And then my church here, I've even gotten him involved in the church in his area. So, we're learning about the same things

Women who exercise some degree of agency and authority appear to more strongly assert their identities as mothers. They often report better quality relationships with their children than mothers who have little or no choice in choosing their children's caregivers. Exercising such authority allows women to make a claim on maternal identity and thus functions as maternal management tool. It can signal to the caregiver and others that a woman is a key player in her children's lives. Further, the ability to identify and help meet a child's needs conveys that a mother is knowledgeable, irreplaceable and that the mother-child bond persists. Though data on the ages of group interview respondents was not collected, women who appeared to be younger in age (estimated to be in their late teens and early twenties) seemed to have far less authority in their children's lives, and to be more comfortable transferring most or all authority to caregivers. Corey, a multi-racial mother, is an example. She gave birth to her only child, a son, while serving her current sentence, and has never provided full-time primary care for him. Her older sister has been raising him since his birth. Corey's comments are informative.

Moderator: Are you consulted about decisions regarding your son?

Corey: No … But she'll do what's best. Like if I want to do something then I'll let her know. She will agree to it. But like … school stuff, she'll make the best decision and … She's real picky and that's the way I want her to be with my son. If it's safe and looks alright and clean …

While Corey is not consulted about decisions regarding her son, she appears comfortable in allowing her sister to perform this role. She also reserves the role of disciplinarian for her sister. While other mothers spoke of grounding, placing children in time-outs or having talks when they misbehaved, Corey said, "He's with me right now …. I hate to see him cry … just let him be a little bad boy … Let him do what he wants." Corey receives very few visits from her son which she attributes to her sister's procrastination. Thus, she prefers that her sister discipline the child, though not in her presence. Nonetheless, the pattern is clear: women who have limited authority are often limited in other aspects of mothering such as discipline and spending time with their children. Though Corey's maternal role is unconventional in many ways, her maternal identity does not seem to be compromised by this arrangement. She views herself as a mother and demonstrates the salience of that identity throughout her narrative.

Getting along: The Impact of Mother-Caregiver Relationships

Upon assuming the responsibility of caring for children, caregivers gain influence in the mother-child relationship. Caregivers can determine the type (visits, letters, phone calls), quality and frequency of interaction between mothers and their children. Essentially, caregivers become gatekeepers of mother-child relationships and greatly influence how mothers perform their role. Among respondents, the quality of the mother-caregiver relationship bespeaks the degree to which caregivers and mothers get along. Women describe good relationships as those in which mothers and caregivers are mutually supportive and work together to pursue the best interest of children. Angel, an African American mother to three sons demonstrates her support for her children's caregiver.

[I] make sure that they … are obeying my mother. If they get in trouble with my mom, she tells me everything and I have a conversation with them and tell them don't do it and they don't do it.

Mothers often offer role support by admonishing their children to comply and cooperate with caregivers. This support seems to be generously offered when caregivers are perceived to possess values and parenting practices that mothers approve. Lindsay, a White mother of three children, demonstrates role support for her mother who cares for her children:

> My mom and I have always been on the same brain wave of discipline ... And my six-year-old tried to tell me, "My Nanna spanked me one day" and I said, if your Nana spanked you, you deserved it ... Right now, she's doing a chart with my six-year-old and when she gets so many stars ... she gets to pick if she wants to go out ... So I agree.

Like many mothers and daughters, Lindsay and her mother hold similar parenting values. Mothers often socialize their daughters for mothering roles, so it is logical that many mother-daughter dyads share parenting practices and ideals. This is apparent among many respondents who report high levels of support for their mothers in their caregiving roles.

Conversely, incarcerated mothers may withdraw support when caregivers do not share their parenting values and practices. Women often assess such caregivers as incompetent and unsupportive of them as mothers. Kris, a White mother of five children, describes a problematic situation with one of her children's caregivers:

> My grandmother has my three [middle] children in California ... She doesn't want to lose them. But she's 82 years old and they tell *her* what to do ... I told her ... you can't keep letting them tell you what to do. I'm going to have to bring them back to ______, and somebody else is going to have to keep them ... And uh, my grandmother is very wealthy ... and I'm not. She ... allows them to get whatever they want ... And I try to tell her that's not good ... because when I come home, I'm not going to be able to buy my children ... they're not going to be able to go to the shelf and pick whatever they want out, because I don't have that kind of money that you have ... You're teaching them that they can have whatever they want in life. And it's not always going to be like that.

Kris doesn't believe her grandmother is capable of providing her children with the boundaries, discipline and structure they need. She also feels that her parenting values are undermined when her grandmother spoils the children and spares them from the reality of what life will be like when Kris resumes care. As a result, she withdraws support. Capitalizing upon her grandma's fear of losing the children, Kris threatens to remove them from her care. Given that an 82-year-old is presently caring for three young children, it seems unlikely that Kris has other caregiver options. Yet it is not possible to know whether Kris' perceived agency is feigned, imagined or real. However, it is clear from other women's narratives that the level of authority Kris implies is far more extreme than what other respondents experience. For most women, caregivers seem to wield the greatest power in the mother-child-caregiver triad. Yet Kris's narrative is noteworthy, reminding us that perceptions, meaning, narratives and perhaps even memories about mothering, are constructed by individuals within the context of the group. These dynamics, even at the extreme, are part and parcel to understanding more about how incarcerated women manage their role-identities.

Though the role support mothers offer to caretakers is important, the support that caregivers can offer, or withhold appears to be far more influential to women's identities and mother-child relationships. Caregivers who offer role support to incarcerated mothers recognize them as viable mothers, rather than absentee parents. Supportive caregivers acknowledge and advocate a mother's role with children and institutions (i.e. schools) as an active authority figure, nurturer, emotional support, as well as other conventional dimensions of motherhood. Birdie, an African American mother of two, describes a situation involving her caregiving sister and her daughter:

> I told my daughter ... I don't want you to have no little boyfriend until I come home. And she was like, "Well, mom you can't do that." I was like, "I'm your mother." She said, "Well I'll just ask my auntie." So, my sister said, "... what did your mother say?" And she said, "Well, my mom said I couldn't have a boyfriend until she comes home." [My sister] said, "Well that's final."

While some caregivers offer role support only on occasion, mothers suggest that quality relationships with caregivers are marked by regular and consistent support. Mothers feel most supported when caregivers regularly allow children to visit and participate in family programs at the prison. These events provide opportunities for mothers and children to reacquaint, bond and experience some similitude of normal family life. Mothers also describe supportive caregivers as those that encourage children to write letters and allow them to have regular phone contact with their mothers as a means of maintaining quality relationships. Mother-child contact has been found to influence mothering attitudes among incarcerated women (Barnes & Stringer, 2014).

Strategies for Maintaining Good Relationships with Caregivers: Cooperation and Communication

Though role support should ideally be reciprocal, mothers acknowledge that the burden of maintaining good relationships with their children's caregivers largely falls upon them. Before becoming incarcerated many of the women in the study were unaccustomed to consulting other persons regarding their children. Thus, learning to compromise with caregivers is a challenge. V, who describes herself as selfish with her children says:

> I have been in that situation [with my children's caregiver] where … you really don't have a say so. And that's what makes it hard because I like to be in control of everything, especially pertaining to my children.

Women described cooperation as the degree to which a caregiver is willing to work together to make major decisions about their children. Though cooperation is by definition reciprocal, many mothers find that they must do most of the yielding in order to maintain a good relationship with caregivers. For instance, V continues:

> … In a situation like this … you have to agree to disagree. Give your side of the situation. Maybe you can come to a mutual agreement. I didn't want my daughter to go to Alabama with her father. But [her caregiver] was like, "If her daddy come over here, I'm not gone [sic] keep her away from her daddy" … It's hard to still be a mama and be up in here.

Like V, mothers can feel like they are at the mercy of their children's caregivers when it comes to their mothering roles. Working with non-familial caregivers can often present an additional challenge. Janise, a White mother, battled with her son's adoptive mother for 1 year before learning to cooperate. Janise relays:

> She could have just taken him. But instead, after fighting for a year and threatening the judges and everything over it, we made friends. Now [my son] visits and I just signed him over to her …

Open communication is also key to maintaining good relationships with their children's caregivers. Respondents described good communication as openness on the part of caregivers to communicate about issues and events that transpire with their children. Most mothers want to be informed on the day-to-day details of their children's lives. Christa, an African American mother says:

> I keep in contact with my mom. I probably call her once a week and she lets me know what my two-year old is doing … I mean you know she keeps me pretty posted on … what they do …

Several mothers attribute their enhanced ability to communicate and have positive relationships with caregivers to the parenting classes they take in the prison's family program. For example, Andrea, a relatively young Hispanic mother of one son speaks about her initial difficulty in communicating with her child's caregiver. She says:

> The people that take care of my child, they're businesspeople and they're always out of town and traveling so, it's like I found it hard to like ask them to bring my son more often cause I feel like they did already too much. The classes I have taken has [sic] helped me to communicate with them more than [I] used to …

Breakdowns in communication and cooperation can create anxiety, frustration and fewer mothering opportunities for sample mothers. Shaleah, a White mother of two explains:

> ... I write my son a letter every week and [his father] won't write me back to tell me how he's doing ... He likes to move and not tell my family where he moves. So now it's like a cat and mouse game.

Here, women's narratives suggest that role support is not always reciprocated by children's caregivers. Respondents often reported perceptions that their children's fathers are the least supportive caregivers. Women's narrative accounts of their frustration, anger and sadness regarding a lack of support from their children's caregivers make clear that these experiences are damaging to a mother's role-identity.

Something to Prove

For women dealing with incarceration, addiction and trauma, mothering can feel like "an all or nothing ultimatum (p. 59)." Thus, mothers may feel the need to prove to themselves, their children, as well as social audiences that they are "good" mothers. (Enos, 2001; Von Weller et al., 2018, p. 59). Mothers who find themselves in difficult circumstances may make comparisons between themselves and others as a means of preserving and negotiating their own maternal identities (Bemiller, 2005). According to McQueeney (2009), women make claims on motherhood to persuade others that they are morally deserving. Among moms in the sample, a strategy used to prove maternal fitness and preserve the maternal identity is the comparison of themselves to their children's caregivers. For many, these comparisons affirm their identity, even when contradictions in their narratives seem apparent. For others, the comparison of themselves to their children's caregivers and other mothers finds them lacking by their own accounts. In these cases, maternal identity may be attenuated. Conversely, comparisons can frame *caregivers* as unfit, a designation that seems to be reserved for caregivers with whom mothers have poor relationships and receive little support. For instance, Dee Dee concedes that her child's father, the primary caregiver, is active in her daughter's life. Yet, she judges him as deficient in his paternal role. Though this may seem like a contradiction, she explains,

> He's active in her life twenty-four hours a day ... but he's not a good father to her because she's not stable ... they look down on me because I'm incarcerated, and I have a drug problem ... But my thing is he's a whore .... He sleeps around and my baby is being drug from here to there ... My child aint on Medicaid .... You know, you're lacking in the areas where she needs things ... Why come she ain't in no daycare? ... She's too smart for you not to have her in school. Ok she hangs around adults twenty-four hours a day. Where's the kids at? ... She's not getting nothing other than street knowledge ... from adults.

By identifying her husband's deficiencies, Dee Dee demonstrates to her social audience as well as herself that she is a good mother. Further, when compared to her husband, *she* is the competent parent who knows how to provide stability, protection, education and appropriate socialization for her child. Though Dee Dee discloses during interviews that she struggles with addiction and is currently serving time for a prostitution case, this does not seem to disqualify her as a mother. She affirms her maternal role-identity by being knowledgeable of what good parents do and provide for their children. Being knowledgeable about their children and childrearing in general becomes evidence in women's case to prove that they are worthy mothers. Likewise, when sample mothers see themselves as meeting prescribed maternal expectations, or as having done so in the past, their maternal identity is affirmed.

Still other women view themselves, rather than others as deficient. When women don't feel that they measure up to social expectations, the maternal identity can be diminished. This can lead women to relinquish the maternal role and may be more likely when mothers believe that caregivers as more competent and capable parents. Kayla, a White mother of four admits:

> I lived a drug life. And I'm not saying just as a user, but a lot of drugs back in my home ... I chose that it was just best that my children were not around me ... My daughter is 17. She asked me when she was about 12 years old, she said, Mom, please don't make me choose between you and dad, because that's what I'll have to do. And I didn't make her choose. I made the choice because I didn't want to hurt my child that way. I'd rather stay out of her life. I'm not going to have my child put through, so I stay out of it.

> She's got college, she's got everything. She doesn't need me. She might need the love of a mother but doesn't need my lifestyle. She's better off where she's at.

Beonka, thinking about her addiction, maternal failures and perceived powerlessness also feels that she doesn't measure up:

> I can give advice. And I can be an example. This (motioning to indicate the prison) is what happens if you step out of line. But other than that, there's nothing I can do ... I haven't been a good example in the past. Those kids aren't stupid. They know what I was doing ... I used to say, "Do as I say, don't do as I do," but you see what I'm doing ... That's why I said I have to be an example. This is what happens.

Beonka relays that because of what she sees as her repeated moral and maternal failings, her oldest daughter has emerged as the mother of their family. Beonka believes that her daughter measures up to motherhood more so than she does. As such, she appears to resign herself to the role of a dependent rather than a mother. Beonka continues,

> She's ... 19 ... She's got the mind of a woman for such a young child. She's very intelligent, she's very mature. She takes care of [my mother]. She's mama to my little girl. The little girl don't like it, but she has to answer to her. When I look at it, she has more sense than I do because [of how] she's carrying herself ...

The narratives of Kayla and Beonka demonstrate that mothering is not being romanticized among respondents. Their narratives also demonstrate Bruner's (1998) point that within narratives we find retrospective interpretations of past choices and events that help to make sense of the present. While many women experience hard won victories in the journey of mothering while incarcerated, some women, in their own estimations, do not measure up. In such cases, instead of managing motherhood, women may relinquish their identities and their parenting role to others whom they perceive to be more capable. In thinking about the sample mothers whose maternal identities were diminished, one cannot help but think about the ways in which conventional ideas about maternity can be harmful and set unrealistic expectations about what motherhood can and should be. For instance, Kayla's belief that her daughter is better off without her could be an impediment to her recovery as well as lead to other harmful behaviors and experiences for both mother and daughter.

CONCLUSION

While a mother's incarceration can separate her from her children, it does not necessarily mean the end of motherhood. Women in this study care deeply for their children and continue to perform and identify as mothers. Rather than the antitheses of mothering, many women are resilient and determined to mother their children. Though the small convenience sample limits the generalizability of the findings, mothers' narratives enhance our understanding of what it means to mother in a carceral context. Most participants continue to identify as mothers and work to manage the mothering role-identity in concert with their children's caregivers. While previous studies document the challenges of mothering while incarcerated (Enos, 2001; Clark, 1995; Thompson & Harm, 2000; Young & Smith, 2000) this study enhances our understanding about some of the strategies women employ to manage their role-identities as mothers while imprisoned. These strategies include making living arrangements for their children, working to maintain quality relationships through cooperation, communication and a willingness to support their children's caregivers. These women are on a mission to prove that they are good mothers despite their past mistakes and misfortunes.

A theoretical framework of mothering roles and identity (role-identity) is useful for framing women's management of the mothering role in a non-normative space like prison. Women's narratives demonstrate a desire to measure up to both personal and social expectations of motherhood. This bespeaks the salience of the maternal identity in many women's lives. However, a smaller group of mothers like Kayla and Beonka, seem to have all but given up on mothering one or more of their children. Yet, women's stories illuminate the ways in which they can use personal agency, however limited, to influence and remain active in the lives of their children. Women's agency is tempered not just by the prison structure itself, but also by caregivers whose opinions and support matter greatly to mothers behind bars.

Group interviews lift and center women's voices and lead to an in-depth understanding of women's experiences. Women's narratives reveal biographical sketches of their lives and relationships with their children and caregivers. Moreover, group interviews reveal how the narrative itself can become a tool for identity management. In Kris's narrative about her children's 82-year old caregiver and her threat to make other living arrangements for them, the narrative itself appears to be used as a tool for Kris to present herself as a mother with unrequited authority and power to command the affairs of her children. Likewise, among other mothers who speak about their children's living arrangements, it becomes clear that the power to choose and approve their children's caregivers is key to managing motherhood while behind bars. This strategy is crucial since caregivers act as gatekeepers to mother-child relationships, and can facilitate or inhibit a mother's engagement and bond with her children. The degree to which women feel valued and supported by caregivers can determine how they function and identify as mothers. Caregivers who support mothers in their roles can simultaneously help solidify the maternal identity. Caregivers who are perceived as unwilling to extend maternal support are the source of significant role strain, which can, in turn, destabilize the mothering role-identity.

Women also strategically use comparison as a means of proving their competence in their roles as mothers. While society and children's caregivers may view incarcerated women as unfit to parent, women are not passive consumers of these labels. Having some authority, possessing knowledge about their children, the ability to discern children's needs and knowing what it takes to be a good parent empowers many women to believe, "I am enough" when it comes to mothering their children. This positive trend among some mothers may be in no small part owing to the prison's family program. The program emphasizes the needs of children, a child-centered lifestyle, parental bonding, effective discipline techniques, family communication, budgeting and other family life skills. Thus, women's resolve to maintain their role-identities despite difficulty and contradiction may be an indication of how family programs can support positive maternal identities.

While this study is informative and effectual in augmenting the knowledge we have about incarcerated mothers' experiences, it has its limitations. Namely, the findings are based on a purposive convenience sample of 55 women. These women may not be representative of the prison itself, or incarcerated women in general. Yet, a range of experiences is represented among sample mothers. While some mothers boast great successes in mothering while incarcerated, others have fledgling maternal role-identities. This is evidence that sample mothers are not merely romanticizing their experiences. As such, there is a healthy confidence in the validity of the findings.

In the prison population from which the sample was drawn, 18% of women report that parental rights to their children have already been terminated while 25% do not expect to have custody of their children upon release. What, if any, are the collateral consequences of permanent social and legal separation for incarcerated mothers and children? Can these relationships be preserved for the benefit of both mothers and children? What role can proxy caregivers play in enhancing the lives of children and mothers? These and other questions must be empirically investigated to discern the best way forward for programs and policies that target incarcerated mothers and their families.

In addition, correctional institutions in America must universally commit to progressive, evidence-based rehabilitation for incarcerated women. Most incarcerated mothers will eventually return to their communities. Given the central role that many women play in their families, prisons must pledge to provide women with the services and skills they need to be better as individuals, but also better family members (Peterson et al., 2018). Findings suggest that incarcerated women, their children and their children's caregivers need access to programs that: teach and encourage healthy family communication; promote positive co/parenting; and provide opportunities to create healthy and meaningful relationships in difficult circumstances. Programs must acknowledge that a mother's incarceration does not in and of itself place children and families at risk, but also poverty, mental illness and a lack of social support for these conditions are also culprits (Peterson et al., 2018; Turney & Wildeman, 2015). Programs must address these precipitating issues to effectively restore families and communities. Programs must also develop inclusive curriculums that reflect the various parenting styles and realities of the women they serve. While intensive mothering indicates a significant investment of time, money and emotional labor into childrearing (Hays, 1996), justice-involved women have historically been marginalized by race, gender inequities and class. Thus, they tend to lack access to the social supports required for these mothering models (Collins, 1994, 2000; Hays, 2003). Further, women in prison are disproportionately racial ethnic minorities whose cultures often emphasize mothering attributes that differ from convention (Collins, 1994). For instance, single African American mothers may emphasize protection and teaching children to be self-reliant rather than dependent upon parents or other caretakers (Elliott et al., 2015). Effective programs must take into consideration these and various other intersecting identities that locate women in the social matrix (Collins, 2000). Failure to do so makes women and children more vulnerable. For instance, Lanctôt and Turcotte (2018) found that justice involved women may seek to distance themselves from deviant labels by pursing normative mothering ideals that present them as "good moms." This leads to role strain and isolation as women with parenting struggles are reluctant to seek support for fear of being judged as a bad mother. Rather than reinforce cultural prescriptions of a "one size fits all" model of motherhood, a restorative justice approach encourages mothers to capitalize on their strengths and implement strategies that can make their children, families and communities whole. This is necessary if prisons are to become sites of positive transformation for incarcerated women rather than contribute to parental isolation and family dysfunction. Though women are influenced by conventional maternity, mothers demonstrate through their narratives that there are different ways to approach motherhood from prison. Yet having the will and resolve to mother their children is not enough. The current study affirms claims by Burke (1991) and Stets & Tsushima (2001) that role support is critical. Thus, if mothers are to be successful in managing their maternal roles and relationships with their children, they will likely need caregiver as well as institutional support to do so.

REFERENCES

Aiello, B. (2016). Making mothers: Parenting classes in a women's jail. *Contemporary Justice Review*, *19*(4), 445–461. https://doi.org/10.1080/10282580.2016.1226819

Aiello, B., & McQueeney, K. (2019). I always thought I was a good mother: Intensive mothering in a women's jail. *Sociological Imagination*, *54*(4), 26–42.

Altheide, D. L. (2004). Ethnographic content analysis. In M. S. Lewis-Beck, A. Bryman, & T. F. Liao (Eds.), *The Sage encyclopedia of social science research methods* (pp. 3260–3270). SAGE.

Baldwin, L. (Ed.). (2015). *Mothering justice: Working with mothers in criminal and social justice settings*. https://ebookcentral.proquest.com

Baldwin, L., Atherton, S., & Thompson, C. (2015). Policing mothers: Intervention, protection and prevention. In L. Baldwin (Ed.), *Mothering justice: Working with mothers in criminal and social justice settings* (pp. 89–112). Waterside Press. https://ebookcentral.proquest.com

Barnes, S. L., & Stringer, E. C. (2014). Is motherhood important? Imprisoned women's maternal experiences before and during confinement and their postrelease expectations. *Feminist Criminology*, *9*(1), 3–23. https://doi.org/10.1177/1557085113504450

Baunach, P. J. (1985). *Women in prison*. Transaction Publications.

Bemiller, M. L. (2005). *Mothering on the margins: The experience of noncustodial mothers* [Unpublished PhD thesis]. University of Akron: Department of Sociology.

Biddle, B. J. (1986). Recent developments in role theory. *Annual Review of Sociology*, *12*(1), 67–92. https://doi.org/10.1146/annurev.so.12.080186.000435

Bloom, B., & Brown, M. (2011). Motherhood on the margins. In J. M. Lawston & A. E. Lucas (Eds.), *Razor wire women: Prisoners, activists, scholars, and artists*. State University of New York Press.
Bloom, B., & Steinhart, D. (1993). *Why punish the children? A reappraisal of the children of imprisoned mothers in America*. National Council on Crime and Delinquency.
Boudin, K. (1998). Lessons from a mother's program prison: A psychological approach supports women and their children. *Women & Therapy, 21*(1), 103–125. https://doi.org/10.1300/J015v21n01_01
Boyd, C. J. (1989). Mothers and daughters: A discussion of theory and research. *Journal of Marriage and the Family, 51*(2), 291–301. https://doi.org/10.2307/352493
Bromberg, E. (1983). Mother-daughter relationships in later life: The effect of quality relationships on mutual aid. *Journal of Gerontological Social Work, 6*(1), 75–92. https://doi.org/10.1300/J083V06N01_07
Brown, M., & Bloom, B. (2009). Reentry and renegotiating motherhood: Maternal identity and success on parole. *Crime & Delinquency, 55*(2), 313–336. https://doi.org/10.1177/0011128708330627
Bruner, J. S. (1998). *Acts of meaning*. Harvard University Press.
Bryman, A. (2004). *Social research methods* (2nd ed.). Oxford University Press.
Burke, P. (1991). Identity process and social stress. *American Sociological Review, 56*(6), 836–849. https://doi.org/10.2307/2096259
Clark, J. (1995). The impact of the prison environment on mothers. *The Prison Journal, 75*(3), 306–329. https://doi.org/10.1177/0032855595075003004
Collins, P. H. (1994). Shifting the center: Race, class, and feminist theorizing about motherhood. In E. N. Glenn, G. Chang, & L. R. Forcey (Eds.), *Mothering ideology experience and agency* (pp. 45–65). Routledge.
Collins, P. H. (2000). *Black feminist thought: Knowledge, consciousness, and the politics of empowerment*. Routledge.
Crawford, J. (2003). Alternative sentencing necessary for female inmates with children. *Corrections Today, 65*(3), 8–10.
Drug Policy Alliance. (2016, February). *Fact sheet: Women, prison, and the drug war*. Drug Policy Alliance. https://www.drugpolicy.org/sites/default/files/DPA_Fact%20Sheet_Women%20Prison%20and%20Drug%20War%20%28Feb.%202016%29.pdf
Elliott, S., Powell, R., & Brenton, J. (2015). Being a good mom: Low-income, black single mothers negotiate intensive mothering. *Journal of Family Issues, 36*(3), 351–370. https://doi.org/10.1177/0192513X13490279
Enos, S. (2001). *Mothering from the inside: Parenting in a women's prison*. State University of New York Press.
Freudenberg, N., Daniels, J., Crum, M., Perkins, T., & Richie, B. E. (2008). Coming home from jail: The social and health consequences of community reentry for women, male adolescents, and their families and communities. *American Journal of Public Health, 98*(Supplement_1), S191–S202. https://doi.org/10.2105/AJPH.98.Supplement_1.S191
Geiger, B., & Fischer, M. (2003). Female repeat offenders negotiating identity. *International Journal of Offender Therapy and Comparative Criminology, 47*(5), 496–515. https://doi.org/10.1177/0306624X03253025
Glaze, L. E., Maruschak, L. M. (2010). *Parents in prison and their minor children*. U.S. Department of Justice, Bureau of Justice Statistics. http://www.bjs.gov/content/pub/pdf/pptmc.pdf.
Glenn, E. N., Chang, G., & Forcey, L. R. (1994). *Mothering: Ideology, experience, and agency*. Routledge.
Goffman, E. (1961). *Asylums: Essays on the social situation of mental patients and other inmates*. Anchor Books.
Green, S., Haney, C., & Hurtado, A. (2000). Cycles of pain: Risk factors in the lives of imprisoned mothers and their children. *The Prison Journal, 80*(1), 3–23. https://doi.org/10.1177/0032885500080001001
Greenburg, R. (2006). Children and families: Mothers who are incarcerated. *Women & Therapy, 29*, 165–179.
Greenfield, L. A., & Snell, T. (1999). *Women offenders*. US Department of Justice. https://www.bjs.gov/content/pub/pdf/wo.pdf
Grief, G. L. (1985). *Single fathers*. Heath and Company.
Gubrium, J. F., & Holstein, J. A. (1997). *The new language of the qualitative method*. Oxford University Press.
Hairston, C. F. (1999). Kinship care when parents are incarcerated. In J. P. Gleeson & C. F. Hairston (Eds.), *Kinship care: Improving practice through research* (pp. 189–212). Child Welfare League of America.
Hairston, C. R. (2007). *Focus on children of incarcerated parents, an overview of the research literature*. A Report for the Annie E. Casey Foundation. http://www.f2f.ca.gov/res/pdf/FocusOnChildrenWith.pdf
Harrison, P. M., & Beck, A. J. (2006). *Prisoners in 2005*. Bureau of Justice Statistics, U.S. Department of Justice.
Hays, S. (1996). *The cultural contradictions of motherhood*. Yale University Press.
Hays, S. (2003). *Flat broke with children: Women in the age of welfare reform*. Oxford University Press.
Henriques, Z. W. (1982). *Imprisoned mothers and their children: A descriptive and analytical study*. University Press of America.
Hill, R. (2003). *The strengths of black families* (2nd ed.). University Press of America.
Ingram-Fogel, C. (1993). Hard time: The stressful nature of incarceration for women. *Issues in Mental Health Nursing, 14*(4), 367–377. https://doi.org/10.3109/01612849309006900
Iskikian, A. (2019). The sentencing judge's role in safeguarding the parental rights of incarcerated individuals. *Columbia Journal of Law and Social Problems, 53*(1), 133–166.

James, W. (1968). The self. In C. Gordon & K. Gergen (Eds.), *The self in social interaction* (pp. 41–49). John Wiley.
Johnston, D. (1997). The care and placement of prisoners' children. In K. Gabel & D. Johnston (Eds.), *Children of incarcerated parents* (pp. 103–123). Lexington Books.
Kendall, D. E. (2012). *Sociology in our times: The essentials*. Wadsworth Publishing.
Kerlinger, F. N. (1964). *Foundations of behavioral research*. Holt, Rhinehart, and Winston.
Lanctôt, N., & Turcotte, M. (2018). The 'good mother' struggles: Obstacles to the attainment of motherhood ideals among adult women formerly placed in residential care. *Child & Family Social Work*, *23*(1), 80–87. https://doi.org/10.1111/cfs.12386
Lombroso, C., Ferrero, G., & Morrison, W. D. (1895). *The female offender*. D. Appleton.
Loper, A. B., & Clarke, C. N. (2013). Attachment representations of imprisoned mothers as related to child contact and the caregiving alliance: The moderating effect of children's placement with maternal grandmothers. *Monographs of the Society for Research in Child Development*, *78*(3), 41–56. https://doi.org/10.1111/mono.12020
Mangus, A. R. (1957). Role theory and marriage counseling. *Social Forces*, *35*(3), 200–209. https://doi.org/10.2307/2573502
Margolies, J. K., Kraft-Stolar, T. (2006). When "Free" means losing your mother. The Collision of Child Welfare and the Incarceration of Women in New York State. A report of the women in prison project of Correctional Association of New York. https://repositories.lib.utexas.edu/bitstream/handle/2152/15159/When_Free_Rpt_Feb_2006.pdf?sequence=2
Maxwell, J. A. (2009). Designing a qualitative study. In L. Bickman & D. J. Rogs (pp. 214–253). *Handbook of applied social science research methods*. Sage Publications.
McCall, G., & Simmons, J. L. (1966). *Identities and interactions*. Free Press.
McGowan, B., & Blumenthal, K. I. (1978). *Why punish the children? A study of the children of women prisoners*. National Council on Crime and Delinquency. https://doi.org/10.1093/sw/24.4.353-a
McQueeney, K. (2009). "We are god's children, y'all:" Race, gender, and sexuality in lesbian- and gay-affirming congregations. *Social Problems*, *56*(1), 151–173. https://doi.org/10.1525/sp.2009.56.1.151
Merlo, A. V., & Pollock, J. (2006). *Women, law and social control*. Allyn and Bacon.
Morash, M., Bynum, T. S., & Koons, B. A. (1998). Women offenders, programming needs and promising approaches. *National Institute of Justice Research in Brief*. U.S. Department of Justice.
Morgan, D. L., & Schwalbe, M. (1990). Mind and self in society: Linking social structure and social cognition. *Social Psychology Quarterly*, *53*(2), 148–164. https://doi.org/10.2307/2786676
Morton, J. B., & Williams, D. M. (1998). Mother/child bonding. *Corrections Today*, *60*, 98–103.
Peterson, W. E., Armstrong, L. L., & Foulkes, M. A. (Eds.). (2018). *Mothers, addiction, and recovery: Finding meaning through the journey*. https://ebookcentral.proquest.com
Philips, S. D., & Gleeson, J. P. (2007). *Children, families and the criminal justice system, a research brief*. Center for Social Policy and Research, University of Illinois.
Poehlmann, J. (2005a). Incarcerated mothers' contact with children, perceived family relationships, and depressive symptoms. *Journal of Family Psychology*, *19*(3), 350–357. https://doi.org/10.1037/0893-3200.19.3.350
Poehlmann, J. (2005b). Representations of attachment relationships in children of incarcerated mothers. *Child Development*, *76*(3), 679–696. https://doi.org/10.1111/j.1467-8624.2005.00871.x
Poehlmann, J., Dallaire, D., Loper, A. B., & Shear, L. D. (2010). Children's contact with their incarcerated parents: Research findings and recommendations. *American Psychologist*, *65*(6), 575–598. https://doi.org/10.1037/a0020279
Poehlmann, J., Shlafer, R. J., Maes, E., & Hanneman, A. (2008). Factors associated with young children's opportunities for maintaining family relations during maternal incarceration. *Family Relations*, *57*(3), 267–280. https://doi.org/10.1111/j.1741-3729.2008.00499.x
Raimon, M., Lee, A., & Genty, P. (2009). Sometimes good intentions yield bad results: ASFA's effect on incarcerated parents and their children. In *Intentions and results: A look back at the Adoption and Safe Families Act* (pp. 121–129). Urban Institute. https://www.urban.org/research/publication/intentions-and-results-look-back-adoption-and-safe-families-act
Schram, P. J. (1999). An exploratory study of stereotypes about mothers in prison. *Journal of Criminal Justice*, *27*(5), 411–426. https://doi.org/10.1016/S0047-2352(99)00013-6
Scott, M. B., & Lyman, S. M. (1968). Accounts. *American Sociological Review*, *33*(1), 46. https://doi.org/10.2307/2092239
Sentencing Project. (2012). *Parents in prison*. https://www.sentencingproject.org/publications/parents-in-prison/
Sentencing Project. (2019, June). *Incarcerated women and girls*. https://www.sentencingproject.org/publications/incarcerated-women-and-girls/
Smith, G. T. (2006). Adoption and safe families act of 1997 and its impact on prisoner mothers and their children. In R. Immarigeon (Ed.), *Women and girls in the criminal justice system: Policy issues and practice strategies*. Civic Research Institute.
Snell, T. L., & Morton, D. (1994). *Women in prison*. Bureau of Justice Statistics.

Stets, J. E., & Burke, P. J. (2000). Negative emotions and coping responses within identity control theory. *Social Psychology Quarterly*, *63*(3), 224–237. https://doi.org/10.2307/2695870

Stets, J. E., & Tsushima, T. M. (2001). Negative Emotion and Coping Responses within Identity Control Theory. *Social Psychology Quarterly*, *64*(3), 283-295. http://dx.doi.org.ezaccess.libraries.psu.edu/10.2307/3090117

Stringer, E. C., & Barnes, S. L. (2012). Mothering while imprisoned: The effects of family and child dynamics on mothering attitudes. *Family Relations*, *61*(2), 313–326. https://doi.org/10.1111/j.1741-3729.2011.00696.x

Stryker, S. (1980). *Symbolic interactionism: A social structural version*. Benjamin/Cummings.

Thompson, P. T., & Harm, N. J. (2000). Parenting from prison: Helping children and mothers. *Issues in Comprehensive Pediatric Nursing*, *23*(2), 61–81. https://doi.org/10.1080/01460860050121402

Travis, J., & Solomon, A. (2003). *Families left behind*. Urban Institute. https://www.urban.org/research/publication/families-left-behind

Turner, J. (1991). *The structure of sociological theory* (6th ed.). Wadsworth Publications.

Turney, K. (2018). Adverse childhood experiences among children of incarcerated parents. *Children and Youth Services Review*, *89*, 218–225. https://doi.org/10.1016/j.childyouth.2018.04.033

Turney, K., & Wildeman, C. (2015). Detrimental for some? Heterogeneous effects of maternal incarceration on child wellbeing. *Criminology & Public Policy*, *14*(1), 125–156. https://doi.org/10.1111/1745-9133.12109

Von Weller, C., Joplin, J., Pecchio, S., Jacobi, T., Miller, K., & Willkomm, L. (2018). Mothering through addiction and jail. In W. E. Patterson, L. L. Armstrong, & M. A. Foulkes (Eds.), *Mothers, addiction, and recovery: Finding meaning through the journey* (pp. 49–66). Demeter Press.

Young, D. S., & Smith, C. J. (2000). When moms are incarcerated: The needs of children, mothers, and caregivers. *Families in Society: The Journal of Contemporary Social Services*, *81*(2), 130–141. https://doi.org/10.1606/1044-3894.1007

Creating and Undoing Legacies of Resilience: Black Women as Martyrs in the Black Community Under Oppressive Social Control

Leah Iman Aniefuna, M. Amari Aniefuna, and Jason M. Williams

ABSTRACT
This paper contextualizes the struggles and contributions of Black motherhood and reproductive justice under police surveillance in Baltimore, Maryland. We conducted semi-structured interviews with mothers regarding their experiences and perceptions of policing in their community during the aftermath of the police-involved death of Freddie Gray. While the literature disproportionately focuses on Black males, little knowledge is known about the struggles and contributions of Black mothers in matters concerning police brutality and the fight against institutional violence. There still remains the question regarding the role of and impact on Black mothers during matters of institutional violence against Black children. We fill this gap by highlighting narratives and lived knowledges within a Black motherhood perspective. Primary themes show that Black women are subject to terror from police and system agents, they face reproductive justice issues, as they are criminalized as mothers—and are affected mentally, but they employ various resistance strategies that strengthen their resilience. Results indicate that Black women are the backbone and martyrs of their communities, but this comes at a tremendous cost because they remain largely unprotected and subject to immeasurable institutional violence and judgment against their mothering strategies.

> A month after my father-in-law was murdered by the police, she [10-year-old daughter] can't handle it. She became a real rebellion. She wasn't acting right in school. I became pregnant, it got worse. I tried to take her and get her help, it didn't work. They turned everything on me, as far as the law ... I went to the court system, and I begged them for help with my 10-year-old at the time. I said, 'I don't have the experience. I'm not a therapist, I'm not a doctor, I'm not a lawyer, I'm not a judge. Please help me, don't let my child be a statistic.'
>
> **Deborah, 51**

INTRODUCTION

Existing literature has exposed the various forms of oppressive social control of low-income, predominantly Black communities (Anderson, 1999; Brunson, 2007; Rios, 2011); however, the disparate treatment of Black boys and men dominates criminal justice discourse and perpetuates Black male exceptionalism (Butler, 2013). Few studies in existing criminological literature highlight the direct and vicarious trauma that Black women face as a result of violence from police and other state actors that have life changing influence. In fact, much violence against Black women by police officers is typically under-reported, under-prosecuted, and undetected (Jacobs, 2017); this violence includes physical, verbal, and sexual assault. Critical scholars have studied the unique interactions between the justice system and Black women and girls and have uncovered the significant effect of the drug war and police violence on Black women, as well as the complex task of motherhood under state control (Crenshaw et al., 2015; Gabbidon et al., 2011; Jacobs, 2017; Mitchell & Davis, 2019).

Crenshaw (1991, 1996) and the African American Policy Forum (AAPF) began the #SayHerName campaign, which aligns with Crenshaw's scholarship on intersectionality. Since 2014, the #SayHerName campaign has become an interdisciplinary beckoning call amongst Black feminist activists and scholars (Brown et al., 2017; McMurty-Chubb, 2016). Although the hashtag has been memorialized in literature and plastered across social media platforms, the continued silence of mainstream media after countless murders and brutal beatings of Black women and girls by police demonstrates the ongoing necessity for the consistent efforts of AAPF's campaign. The #SayHerName movement underscores the consequences of state violence against Black women and girls. Drawing from existing critical literature (Hill, 2018; James, 1996), we define "state violence" as physical and psychological harm and abuse perpetrated by police and other state actors with life-changing influence. Moreover, state actors include individuals working on behalf of governmental agencies, including child protective services. The present study builds upon the literature and activism aligned with #SayHerName, as we move beyond the normal distribution of a dataset and highlight the narratives of Black women to convey the significance of state violence against Black women.

In calling attention to state violence as a reproductive issue we foreground this study in SisterSong's (2020)[1] call to "analyze power systems" (para 3), and to highlight how "all oppressions impact [black women's] reproductive lives" (para 3). With understanding how all oppressive systems are indicative of reproductive issues, we also submit that for the purposes of this paper reproductive justice is about "a human right to maintain personal bodily autonomy, to have children, not have children, and parent the children we have in safe and sustainable communities" (para 1). Roberts (1997) is in concert with the above mentioned quotes insofar she agrees that the intersecting oppressions Black women face, in particular, are part and parcel of reproductive injustice. Thus, the injustices that Black women face inevitably trickles down onto their already existing children or their children to be, and whatever harms to be done to their children are ultimately heartfelt on Black mothers, too. For Black mothers like Mamie Till (Emmitt Till's mom), SisterSong would lament that she too had a right to see her son grow up. They would further purport that whether eviscerated via state-sanctioned or vigilante violence, the mere unjust erasure of Black children (age notwithstanding) is an affront to reproductive freedoms that Black women have been long denied since the Middle Passage and slavery.

The narratives of the Black women in the present study are the result of in-depth open-ended interviews conducted as part of a critical ethnography and phenomenological study in Baltimore, Maryland. The purpose of this study is to explore Baltimore residents' perceptions and experiences with police following the murder of Freddie Gray[2] and the subsequent protesting throughout

---

[1]We foreground our study in the work of SisterSong, an organization of revolutionary women of color who defined the contours of reproductive justice issues in an effort to highlight the many intersectional issues affecting women of color despite their widespread exclusion from mainstream feminist discourse primarily led by white middle- and upper-class women.

[2]In 2015, the controversial death of Freddie Gray, a 25-year-old Black man, was presumed to be caused by fatal injuries sustained after being beaten while handcuffed and detained by police. Gray succumbed to his injuries while being transported to jail for allegedly carrying a knife. Following his death, the "Baltimore Uprising" occurred, which included organized protests around the city that garnered national attention and attracted participation from people across the country

the city. Consistent with the principles of field research, the study was conducted with a hypothesis under consideration, but was exploratory in nature (Bhattacharya, 2017), especially given the acute nature of the issues under investigation. We found that the Black women interviewed in this sample experienced both direct and vicarious traumatic experiences with the police, especially after calling the police for help. It was also discovered that the Black women in this sample described various forms of oppressive social control perpetrated by the police and other state actors; however, the women regularly employ survival strategies to both avoid and heal from these violent interactions. The primary themes we extracted from our sample of narratives are that Black women are subject to terror from police and system agents, and they face reproductive justice issues, as their mothering strategies are criminalized. The historical preoccupation with stifling Black motherhood (see e.g., Roberts, 1995), in particular, presents a peculiar kind of reproductive justice issue similar to contemporary administration of justice issues. For instance, in the context of this study, disproportionate police brutality against Black youth and adult bodies who are the children of Black women is a heavily understudied area of reproductive justice with which we have found evidence in our sample. This area of reproductive justice is especially dire when victims of said violence are later pronounced deceased. Eponymous symptoms include a decline in these mothers' mental health despite employing various resistance strategies that ground their resilience. Moreover, reproductive justice also becomes a dire consequence when state violence against Black women results in bodily harm that presents irreparable damage to their reproductive organs and when the criminal label or contact with the justice system or the state surveillance apparatus prevents them from being able to find a child-bearing spouse. Thus, results from this study indicate that Black women specifically experience incomparable reproductive justice issues due to the heightened risk of losing their children to police violence or the unwarranted placement into the custody of the state. Despite constantly combating the consequences of state surveillance, our collaborators[3] demonstrate that Black women engage in what Collins (2002) describes as "othermothering,"[4] as they are the backbone and martyrs of their communities, especially in crises, but extant literature show that they remain understudied and unprotected as it pertains to police violence.

In the following sections, we explain our guiding theoretical frameworks of Critical Race Theory (CRT) and Black Feminist Criminology (BFC), which is followed by a brief comparative analysis of the existing feminist criminological theoretical discourses. Then, we corroborate our study with a historical investigation of the striking similarities of 17th and 18th century prisons and the themes found in the narratives. Lastly, we explain our methodological procedures, and we report and analyze the narratives collected.

THEORETICAL FRAMEWORK

We ground our critical ethnographic study in Critical Race Theory (CRT) and Black Feminist Criminology (BFC), which are both rooted in scholarly resistance to oppressive social control mechanisms and were established to fill the gaps of orthodox, colorblind criminology and legal theories (Bell, 1995; Potter, 2006). We apply the frameworks of CRT and BFC to our study,

---

during the highly publicized adjudication process of the several Baltimore Police Department officers involved in the death of Freddie Gray. The officers faced criminal charges but were ultimately not indicted.

[3]We refer to the participants in our study as our collaborators, rather than the common research terminology. We recognize that the invaluable perspectives of the volunteers in our study could not be added to the body of knowledge without their partnership.

[4]Collins (1990) explains the role of "othermothers," (p. 192) as Black mothers within communities sharing mothering responsibilities by helping raise and protect Black children. She demonstrates the importance of othermothers to Black communities and the institution of Black motherhood. We discuss this concept in greater detail and in relation to our collaborators' experiences in later sections of this article.

because they critically examine race and intersectionality in the context of the criminal legal system. Bell (1980, 1995), one of the pioneers of CRT, infiltrates the embedded racism in our society and affirms the matrix between race and power (Crenshaw et al., 1996). In addition, CRT brings awareness to the social structures that create social inequalities and oppression that particularly affect the lives of African Americans (Bhattacharya, 2017). It is essential to first understand the major tenets of CRT, which are the deconstruction of structural oppression, reconstruction for equality of all, and construction with equal power (Schuh et al., 2011). Similarly, BFC breaks down the concerns of the lived experiences of Black women into four themes: social structural oppression, the Black community and culture, intimate and familial relations, and Black women as the individual (Potter, 2006). These nuances are critical to include in a comprehensive analysis of Black women, as such they all have been employed throughout this study.

Although scholars have applied a gendered analysis to CRT, the theory is unable to fully capture the deeply complex nature of Black women's experiences. Therefore, BFC was created as a rigorous extension to CRT and to fill the gaps of orthodox criminology, which completely devalues the significance regarding the combination of multiple marginalized identities, such as race, skin color, sex, gender identity, socio-economic status, sexual orientation, disability, and religion.[5] Applying CRT and BFC to the phenomenon of state violence against Black women is essential because of their unique experiences with the justice system in comparison to other women. Additionally, our analysis is informed by more nuanced components of CRT and BFC, including the theoretical perspective of intersectionality. Orthodox antiracist and feminist theoretical conceptions one-dimensionally examine either race or gender, respectively. Crenshaw (1989), the scholar responsible for coining the term, "intersectionality," declares that Black women are marginalized from both antiracist policy and feminist theory, because the underpinnings of both conceptions are based on experiences that fail to demonstrate the interaction of race *and* gender. The exclusion of Black women's experiences promotes scholarship (and ultimately public acceptance) that invalidates the seriousness of Black women's struggles combating racism, sexism, classism, and any other forms of discrimination simultaneously, which ultimately leads to the erasure of their existence altogether. Intersectionality, as defined by Crenshaw (1991), considers the interactions of racism and patriarchy and describes the marginalized "location" (p. 1265) at which Black women exist because of their exclusion from Black liberation and feminist movements. Theoretical contours that fail to explicitly apply an intersectional[6] perspective perpetuate this scholarly silencing of Black women's voices and discursively agree that the multiplicity of oppression for Black women is insignificant.

BFC is a framework that places Black women's lived experiences at the forefront of examination (Potter, 2006). The necessity for BFC was advocated by criminologist, Hillary Potter (2006), in her seminal article that amplifies the voices of Black women experiencing intimate partner violence. Potter later expanded this framework (2013, 2015), advocating for the application of intersectionality to "disrupt" (Potter, 2015, p. 7) orthodox criminological theory and research, which traditionally excludes Black women from analyses or inappropriately applies theories that fail to capture the intensified consequences of being Black, and a woman in addition to any other marginalized identity. In *Intersectionality and Criminology: Disrupting and Revolutionizing Studies of Crime*, Potter (2015) urges criminologists that the analysis of crime and the administration of justice is incomplete without incorporating intersectionality. Crenshaw (1989) substantiates the

[5]This is not an exhaustive list of identities that impact an individual's lived realities and experiences with police or other state actors. Race, sex, gender identity, socio-economic status, sexual orientation, disability, and religion are typically identified as some of the most salient of an individual's characteristics. We acknowledge that there are many other ways that people identify that are visible and invisible that impact how they are perceived and treated, and ultimately tilts their fulcrum of privilege and oppression in any given situation.

[6]We use the terms "intersectionality" and "intersectional" interchangeably to describe the phenomenon of multiple forms of oppression that Black women experience. In Crenshaw's original conception of the terms, she uses both variations of the term.

establishment of intersectionality with several examples of case law illustrating the state's perpetuation of Black women into an unprotected class within the margins, and she later sharpens the concept with examples of violence against Black women (1991). Similarly, Potter (2013, 2006) establishes and expands on BFC and intersectional criminology after finding evidence of the effect with intimate partner abuse on Black women. Although intersectionality can also be applied to daily encounters of microaggressions, the concept can explain the most egregious forms of abuse and violence against Black women and the subsequent rejection of them as victims. Thus, we center intersectionality in our theoretical foundation because our findings highlight the paradox of being both Black and a woman as a complex identity that can impact how Black women are perceived and treated by police and other state actors.

HISTORICAL CONTEXT

In Du Bois' (1920) notable publication, *Dark Water: Voices from Within the Veil*, the author illustrates the consequences of seeking liberation for Black men while allowing Black women to remain in the margins. Du Bois (1920) warns, "The world that wills to worship womankind studiously forgets its darker sisters" (p. 165). The study of race and crime has universally forgotten the complexities of Blackness for women. For these reasons, CRT and BFC have been created and employed in order to examine these complexities comprehensively.

Young's (2001) study provides a historical context of the relationship between Black women and the system in the Maryland penitentiary. The present study was conducted in Baltimore, so understanding the historical landscape provided by Young's study is paramount. The Maryland penitentiary's pre-Civil War population consisted of 70% Black women and 30% white women; whereas, the post-Civil War population increased to 90% Black women (Young, 2001). Additionally, Black women were segregated from white women in more dehumanizing and restrictive quarters (Young, 2001). Black women were more likely to serve their full sentences and be denied of pardoning procedures than white women who committed similar crimes (Young, 2001). Shortly after, in 1910, Baltimore became the first city in the United States to pass a block-by-block segregation ordinance, which was followed by various other discriminatory practices (United States Department of Justice, 2016). Baltimore's discriminatory laws still systematically affect economic conditions for Black people; as a result, Baltimore is now one of the most segregated cities in America.

The United States Department of Justice (DOJ) (2016) *Investigation of the Baltimore City Police Department* revealed that the 1910 block-by-block ordinance set a precedent for the Baltimore police department to have a focused patrol on the Black blocks, which still exists today. Consistent with the history of these blocks, there are visual disparities of the homes that reside in these areas, which was affirmed via our ethnographic observations. In addition, Baltimore nearly doubles the 12% poverty rate in the United States (United States Census Bureau, 2018). The Baltimore police department takes a broken windows policing approach by projecting a need for more policing of these areas. Nevertheless, although the city deploys more officers in concentrated areas, the DOJ's investigation of the city's police department proves various tactics to be ineffective, violent, and damaging to the city (DOJ, 2016).

The history of the city of Baltimore and the relationship between Black women and the state of Maryland's criminal justice system has glaring issues that can be found in low-income predominantly Black communities across the country (Brunson, 2007). The dominance of white structural and economic power stifle any potential for equal opportunities that Black women may have been afforded otherwise. Instead, the juxtaposition of power and an inherently racist state system pose a threat to the existence of Black women, and by extension, their Black children. Du Bois (1920) explains the history of Black motherhood and the relationship between Black women and the state. He declares that "[Black women] existed not for themselves, but for men. Black women were the breeders of human cattle for the auction block ... welding for its children chains" (Du Bois, 1920, p. 165). Black women's existence and their positions as mothers in the United States has been one of scrutiny and vulnerability for centuries.

LITERATURE REVIEW

Despite gaps in literature concerning the treatment of Black women by police, critical scholars have studied and advocated for the intentional inclusion of Black women in mainstream discourse. This section reviews the existing literature regarding Black women and police terror, consequential issues of Black motherhood and reproductive justice, and various methods of creative survival employed by Black women.

Police Violence and Terror

Although the focus on Black women as victims of police violence and terror is reemerging, the work of critical scholars has historically been underscored by the one-dimensional, "all women" approach that assumes all women have the same experiences. The popular misdiagnosis of paternalism and the chivalry hypothesis have dominated much criminological discourse (Moulds, 1978; Spohn & Beichner, 2000; Steffensmeier & Demuth, 2006), and consequently, Black women are inherently presumed precipitants of the violence against them or incapable of being victimized altogether (Jacobs, 2017).

The DOJ (2016) investigation of the Baltimore City Police Department (BPD) highlights the unconstitutional tactics engrained within the department. Part of the DOJ's investigation found that the BPD regularly uses excessive force on individuals that are most vulnerable, including people with mental illnesses, intellectual disabilities, individuals in crises, and people who pose no threat of harm or imminent danger. Women most often fell into this category of citizens victimized by BPD. The DOJ also highlighted that the BPD has a significant gender bias issue that is normalized within the department and particularly prejudices the investigation of sexual assault claims. During his interview of a woman reporting sexual assault, an officer stated, "Why are you messing that guy's life up" (DOJ, 2016, p. 122), indicating the higher valuation placed on men's lives than women's lives. In another investigation, the DOJ documented that a prosecutor wrote via e-mail, "This case is crazy ... I am not excited about charging it. This victim seems like a conniving little whore (pardon my language)." The BPD officer replied via e-mail: "Lmao! I feel the same" (p. 122). Although the race of the victims in these cases are not provided, the report indicates that the BPD's cases disproportionately involve Black residents, which suggests that Black women are at significant risk for similar dehumanization.

Nonetheless, Jacobs (2017) reports that the DOJ's investigation failed to include the egregious strip search of a Black woman by BPD, which was allegedly perpetrated against her during a traffic stop due to a broken taillight. This violent encounter was not covered by national news, rather via the pages of outraged social media users. Similarly, knowledge of Korryn Gaines' murder and the shooting of her 5-year-old son was televised via live video posted on Gaines' FaceBook page, who recorded the encounter to ensure that the officers responsible for her victimization would be held accountable (Sharpe-Levine, 2019). Consistent with the disregard for Black women's lives, the family's 37 million-dollar award was rescinded by the court despite a jury's decision to award the damages more than a year ago (Jacobs, 2019).

Because of the lack of national outcry for the lives of Black women, social media provides primary access to knowledge of police and vigilante violence against Black women and girls (Hill, 2018). The public tends to learn of the most egregious cases through social media, rather than national headlines reporting the deaths and beatings or subsequent protests. Therefore, awareness is limited to the network that individual users create and choose to consume; hence, affirming the necessity for the #SayHerName movement.

Critical scholars have led the scholarly movement for the study of unique interactions between the justice system and Black women and girls (Crenshaw et al., 2015; Gabbidon et al., 2011). Black feminist theorists compare images of Black women as mammies and matriarchs (Collins, 2002) to police officers' need to control Black women. However, Black women remain understudied and unprotected as it pertains to police violence. Albeit important, contemporary criminological discourse highlights the war on drugs, the explosion of Black male inmates, and the concurrent murders of Black males at the hands of police (Alexander, 2011; Brunson, 2007). Thus, many negative interactions with police documented in existing literature relate to Black women and their children. Aside from physical violence, the natural consequence of policing women is the impact on their children, especially since Black women mother their communities (Collins, 2002; Jones, 1985). The next section explores the complexities of mothering for Black women under oppressive social control.

Black Motherhood and Reproductive Justice

Prior literature depicts the consequences of the criminalization of Black women; therefore, it is essential to discuss Black motherhood as it relates to state control. Police terror and the constant threat of state violence dramatically impacts Black women as individuals and as mothers. Nonetheless, some scholars have uncovered the effect of the drug war and the spike of Black women behind bars, especially as it relates to the complex task of motherhood under state control (Bloom et al., 1994; Jacobs, 2017).

The complexities of state violence, control, and hyper-surveillance are understudied in relation to reproductive justice. Activism and scholarship on reproductive justice applies an intersectional approach to the issues of access and reproductive health, sexual health, and abortion (Zucker, 2014). It is paramount to critically analyze the role of the state, including the legal system, law enforcement, and child protective services, in criminalizing and policing Black mothers in ways that mothers of other races would not endure (Roberts, 1993, 1999). We identify the risk of mothering while Black as a result of criminalizing Black mothers as a reproductive justice issue because of the lived realities of our collaborators.

Davis (1983) describes Black women as "anomalies" (p. 5) because of the strict definitions of femininity juxtaposed to Black women's laborious roles on plantations and as wet nurses. Roberts (1993) simplifies the consequences of this phenomenon as she explains the dynamic matrix of race and gender-based oppression facing Black mothers post-slavery. We rely on Roberts' (1993, 1995, 1997, 1999, 2003, 2012) foundational texts, as she delivers the legal context of the task of Black mothers raising their children while protecting them from the implications of the state's constant pursuit to control and detain Black bodies. Roberts' (1993) work frames our analysis, as she asserts that the white patriarchal construction of motherhood and motherwork inherently criminalizes Black women.

Relatedly, Collins' (2002) conceptualization of Black motherhood is exceptionally fitting for the current study. Black mothers in the US have long deployed mothering strategies reminiscent of those from African cultures that are foregrounded in community-based care. As Collins has articulated, these deployments of motherhood are responses to the intersecting forms of oppression they face as Black women and mothers. There are also qualitative differences in the functionality of Black motherhood, such as, her notion of "othermothers"—those stand-in mothers who are not the biological parent of a child, but nevertheless, a caretaker of the community's children in the absence of the biological parent. While the construction of Black motherhood, in particular, has always been constructed from the gaze of those who have not had to live the intersecting oppressions of Black womanhood, Collins provides a riveting, organic exclamation of what Black motherhood is:

> … motherhood can serve as a site where Black women can express and learn the power of self-definition, the importance of valuing and respecting ourselves, the necessity of self-reliance and independence, and a belief in Black women's empowerment. These tensions foster a continuum of responses. Some women view motherhood as a truly burdensome condition that stifles their creativity, exploits their labor, and makes them partners in their own oppression. Others see motherhood as providing a base for self-actualization, status in the Black community, and a catalyst for social activism. (p. 191)

Collins' description of Black motherhood provides a basis from which to understand the standpoint definition of motherhood from the lived reality of Black women themselves against typically ill-conceived notions designed to conceal the real hardships associated with Black motherwork practices.

Therefore, any woman who falls short of the white-washed, elite conception of a mother is deemed deviant, criminal, and defeminized; for example, unwed mothers, unfit mothers, and women without children. The state has historically attempted to reduce Black women as mothers and fundamentally as women. Jones and Seabrook (2017) refer to the denial of Black women as mothers as the "New Jane Crow," as well as the phenomenon of the systematic seizure of Black children as property of the state. The state has kidnaped Black children as if they are chattel with no emotional relationship or physical connection with their mothers and families (Paltrow, 2012). Contemporary views of Black women as less feminine than white women and undeserving of the label of a women or as a mother are consistent with the history of white women routinely owning plantations filled with slave men, women, and children (Jones-Rogers, 2019). Roberts (2012) declares that the coercive relationship between Black women, their children, the criminal justice system, and the foster care system are interconnected mechanisms to deny the significant contributions of Black women as mothers. However, American history rests on the bosom of Black women, who were required to wet nurse and mother the children of their masters and mistresses, many times after having their own babies abducted from their wombs (Jones-Rogers, 2019).

Gurusami (2019) highlights the labor of Black mothers returning home after incarceration. The author establishes the term "decarceral motherwork" as the intentional resistance of formerly incarcerated mothers against state hyper-supervision interfering with their mothering. Gurusami's (2019) depiction of "hypervigilant motherwork" can be compared to Mullings (1997) illustration of how Black mothers dedicate most of their time to shielding their children from random street violence. Thus, Black mothers redirect their time and energy from any other needs and desires in their lives, as they are expected to singlehandedly or with the help of othermothers (Collins, 1990) shield their children from the state-manufactured threat of losing their children to random street violence (Mullings, 1997) or unwarranted seizure by the child welfare system (Roberts, 2003).

Creative Survival and Resilience

Many other experiences have unique effects on Black people due to the systemic and strategic oppression reinforced by the justice system, which are captured by Russell-Brown (2004) as "living while Black" and operationalized by Gabbidon and Peterson (2006) "Living While Black Index." Despite the horrific annals of Black womanhood and Black motherhood under state control, Black women have found refuge in various outlets, such as religion and spirituality, the arts, and education. Scholars have studied Black women's survival strategies against various sources of trauma, including witnessing community violence (Clark et al., 2008), intersectional oppression (Neal-Barnett & Crowther, 2000), intimate partner violence (Potter, 2007; Ritchie, 1996), and the criminalization of Black motherhood (Mitchell & Davis, 2019; Roberts, 1993). We apply Evans, Bell, Burton, and Blount's (2017) philosophy of Black women's creative survival to criminology to explain the resilience of Black women resisting state violence, the matrix of domination (Collins, 2002), and the distinctive racist, sexist, classist, and homophobic suffering described by (Jones and Guy-Sheftall, 2015) as the "Black girl Blues." Existing literature provides common survival strategies employed by Black women: religion and spirituality, various forms of art, higher education, being self-reliant, exerting their energy into raising their children, being protectors of others (othermothering), and drawing strength from their ancestors (Evans et al., 2017; Everett et al., 2010; Jenkins, 2002; Shorter-Gooden, 2004; St. Vil et al., 2017).

The consequences of incarceration and motherhood have been explored for decades. Very little research qualitatively addresses Black women's experiences with police violence, how Black women persevere through this violence, and motherhood as resistance. Thus, Black women tend to suffer silently and bear their trauma. Despite the perpetual emotional and physical battering of Black women by criminal justice professionals, which we liken to a state-sanctioned "War on Black Women," Black women have certainly proven to persevere, discover creative methods of survival, and still act as martyrs in their communities.

METHODOLOGY

The data for this study is generated from a larger ethnographic study on policing following the Freddie Gray incident in Baltimore. In an effort to explore a gendered analysis, the data from semi-structured interviews was partitioned for specific coding that reflected our research inquiry. This study received IRB approval by the principal investigator's home institution, and various safeguards have been followed to reduce harm and protect the participants of the study (referred to hereafter as collaborators). The central research inquiry was to examine the experiences and perceptions of Black women with the police and other state actors in Baltimore. Further, the study was guided by mixed qualitative methodological framework: phenomenology and critical ethnography. First, the phenomenological approach was employed in order to understand the phenomenon of the interactions between the Black community and police as well as other state actors following the Freddie Gray incident. Phenomenology offers a theoretical lens to understand people's lived experiences of a phenomenon (Bhattacharya, 2017). Our study exclusively focuses on the experiences of Black women with the police, as well as interactions with other state actors. Next, a critical ethnography was conducted, because it was imperative to submerge as an observer-as-participant to explore the lived realities and culture of our collaborators. According to Bhattacharya (2017), critical ethnography is utilized when social impediments such as inequality are both intentionally foregrounded into a study's investigation and readily accepted as reality by the researcher. Nevertheless, this method allowed for the thorough understanding of the surroundings, experiences, and perceptions of our collaborators.

In addition, in-depth open-ended semi-structured interviews ($N = 8$) were conducted to gather information regarding our collaborators' experiences and perceptions around the police and other state actors. The interviews averaged about 35 min each. The sample was gathered via the snowball sampling technique, and it was confirmed that each participant was a resident of Baltimore and 18 years of age or older. After deploying each methodological strategy, the data was triangulated to control for qualitative validity and reliability during the coding process.

In considering reflexivity, it was important to cogitate our positionality to participants and individual social location while taking the role of observer-as-participant. It was essential to the study that the research team consisted of individuals that were of close social proximity[7] to our collaborators. Thus, ensuring that our research team projected a sense of relatability to the subject matter and participants was important and essential for conducting research with this

[7]Our research team consists of a Black woman and two Black men, each of whom are very familiar with the lived realities and complexities of living in communities plagued by hyper-surveillance and racialized police practices.

hard-to-reach population that otherwise may not have participated in such a study. This also allowed greater access into certain gendered spaces and conversations that may not have been openly obtained by an all-male or all-white research team—also adding greater quality to inter-subjectivity inherent in qualitative research. Nonetheless, the psychometric qualities of the instrument were considered to preserve content validity, as the instrument covered a range of interpretations within the topic. The purpose of the semi-structured interview was as follows: to understand our collaborators' experiences and perceptions of police and the criminal justice system prior to the Freddie Gray incident, their opinions of the Freddie Gray incident and their thoughts on how the investigation was conducted, their thoughts more broadly on the system in Baltimore and racial implications, the effects of the Freddie Gray incident on the community and its national impact, their perceptions of community leadership, and lastly, their advice to youth to stay out of the system. Moreover, despite the omission of gender-specific questions, our collaborators innately provided answers from their social locations. Because the methodological approach was phenomenological, some unexpected underlying themes emerged, which guided the direction of the study.

RESULTS

The findings suggest that this sample of Black women in Baltimore have extremely traumatic experiences with the police in their community. The trauma from police terror described by our collaborators mimics the traumatic effects of abuse. Some collaborators described safety as trying to avoid the perpetrators of violence (police), isolating themselves in their homes, attempting to protect their children from cruelty, and "minding their business." Similar to Gurusami's (2019) study, our collaborators were determined to protect their children and the integrity of their motherhood, in spite of the threat posed by the state. Although the study investigates system-imposed trauma, survival strategies and coping mechanisms also mirror victims of other forms of abuse.

Throughout the following section, we report narratives from our collaborators on the three prominent themes: police and system terror of Black women, Black motherhood and reproductive justice, and Black women's mental health and resilience. We also intermittently report the ethnographic findings of our investigation to illustrate the holistic detriment of the community and its peripheral implications on our collaborators.

Police and System Terror of Black Women

As we traveled to the fast food restaurant where we met our collaborators, we observed the lopsided ratio of livable homes to boarded homes. There were several streets in Baltimore characterized by uninhabitable rowhouses, many of which had shattered and boarded windows and doors. Some of the homes did not have doors, altogether; however, families still occupied these decayed homes. There was also a distinct intensification of police presence as we entered the city as opposed to those communities where the number of patrol officers was minimal.

Our collaborators expressed deep fear of dealing with police. Most of our collaborators attempted to avoid the police altogether, which seemed extremely difficult because of the heightened presence. Deborah, who is 51 years old, recounted several instances of her interactions with police and other state actors, which ultimately changed her life. Deborah conveyed the impact of the terror she felt from dealing with police, as she was afraid and felt like a prisoner in her own house. As a result, she often stays in the house in order to avoid dealing with the police:

> So, my experience with the police with them coming into my home. They never asked me questions, they never looked at me, and said well, 'It's a possibility that maybe this child is the one that is rebelling.' You automatically come to my house and snatched my child. You told me I was an unfit mother. You know, you had me going from all these different programs, parenting classes—I am 51 years old. There is nothing

> you can teach me about being a mother. If I don't know that by now, I will never know... But because I love my child so much, I was willing to degrade myself, sitting in here with 18-year olds who don't have a clue about being a mother.

This is one example of the daily terror faced by one of our collaborators, and the way it impinges upon the way they live their lives. Deborah's story is distinct from Collin's (2002) description of Black mothering strategies to some extent. For instance, typically, most Black mothers will try to limit the state's contact with their children, however, the intersecting oppressions she faces are so tremendous that she believed capitulating to the state was her only way to help her child. Meanwhile, she was also keenly aware that it was indeed the state that had allowed her multiple oppressions to persevere.

Janet, who is 70 years old, expressed staying away from white police officers, because of their history of sexual harassment and physical abuse of Black women in Baltimore city. She posits:

> I stayed away from the whites, because the white policeman in Baltimore City back in my day actually, tried to, mostly, hit on black women on the side and—I mean, we went through a lot of that, we did. You stayed away from the white officers, because they were nasty. They wanted to have relations with you on the side, or hurt you or lock you up for nothing, but Black cops who were the ones that I think disappointed me to a certain degree because they seemed to be harder on Black men than the white police officers. Even today, that still exists, you know. So, as a whole with the police department, I think, for Black people in Baltimore, it was more, I don't know, it's a matter of discipline. That's all they wanted to do is discipline us.

Janet's account of avoiding white police officers reveals the perpetual cycle of terror on Black women. Janet echoes the analyses of scholars who have confronted the implications of fetishizing the bodies of Black women (Davis, 1983; Jones-Rogers, 2019). Consistent with other indicators of reproductive justice matters that undoubtedly affect Black mothering, experiences around sexual assault can have long lasting effects on Black women's ability to parent. Moreover, stories like Janet's can also have an effect on trust between Black women and the police, which may lead to a myriad of public safety risks that can put Black women and their children's lives at risk.

A common theme illustrated by our collaborators was a willingness to "deal with crooks and robbers" rather than the police. Tameka, who is 30 years old, conveyed that with "crooks and robbers you know what to expect, but with the police, it is uncertain what you'll get whether they try to physically abuse you, rape you, or kill you," which was echoed by Janet and multiple other collaborators. Collins (2002) laments that Black mothers feel the need to socialize their daughters for a world that does not see and accept them. These processes of socialization often include rejecting the politics of hypersexuality placed upon their bodies—but they also include knowing how to avoid and respond to the sure gravity of violence they are likely to encounter. Elaine, who is 43 years old, vividly detailed an instance of racial profiling that she explained traumatized her three decades earlier, at 13 years old. Contrary to widespread assumptions, Elaine debunked the myth that only Black men and boys suffer the consequences of racial profiling and police harassment:

> I was about 13. I was coming out my building in the projects, and I'm going towards Seven-Eleven. My mother sent me to the store. So police threw me on the wall. Now, remind you, I'm 13 years old. I know nothing about drugs, nothing about none of that. But I got thrown on the wall. Me and some grown adults and neighbor guys. But because I fit a description of another young lady, I fit a description of another young lady that was older than me—I'm 13. This young lady was in her 20s. I got thrown on the wall, disrespected and all this type of stuff.

Although Black mothers have passed down creative survival guides to their daughters throughout generations, these strategies have not, however, stood against the might and power of those institutions (like policing) that have long cemented Black women's subordination to the state and other classes. It did not seem to matter that Elaine was 13 years old at the time of her incident, either. Collins explains that socialization for survival often begins before the child is a preteen.

Another one of our collaborators, Tamia, who is 42 years old, insinuated that the police in Baltimore operate lawlessly. Tamia elaborated:

> See, just because you passed the academy, and you passed the test and everything is looking A-okay and you got that badge, it don't make you God. You understand? You just can't do—you got to follow rules. Everything comes with rules. You just can't do what you want.

Collectively, these Black women are impacted daily by institutional agents of power, and they are constantly fearful of what may happen to them if subject to an interaction with the police. This hinders their ability to exist on their terms, as the subconscious and conscious terror imposed by police pervades their daily routines. As Collins (2002) accentuated, Black mothers must develop creative survival mechanisms through which to survive such encounters, and these strategies are necessarily passed down to their children for the same purposes. Whether they have had direct or vicarious experiences with the police, our collaborators' narratives regarding police legitimacy and unconstitutional practices echoes the DOJ's (2016) findings during their investigation of the Baltimore Police Department. Also, the narratives above underscore the extent to which perceived police terror impacts Black motherhood. The constant threat of state intervention invalidates their authority as mothers.

Black Motherhood and Reproductive Justice

Each of our collaborators are mothers, and for some, their negative experiences with police occurred when caring for their children. Our collaborators' insight conveys that motherhood is used as a tool to control Black women. The ways in which Black women parent their children are policed, and they are punished erroneously, especially when seeking resources to help parent their children more effectively. This poses a reproductive justice threat to Black mothers, who are consequently unable to mother their children healthily and safely. The daily terror experienced from the police by Black women potentially puts their children at risk of being entangled in the system, homeless, or at risk of suffering from mental health abnormalities. These types of outcomes are due to risks of incarceration when dealing with the police or other state actors, specifically when our collaborators are sole providers and caretakers for their homes. Deborah conveyed constantly seeking help for her daughter, who kept running away after losing her grandfather, who was beaten to death by the police. She called the police out of desperation to get help for her daughter, and the police turned the blame on her, proclaiming she was an unfit mother. Subsequently, Deborah was forced to take a parenting class at 51 years old, where she was surrounded by young, teenage mothers. Deborah shared the humiliating feeling she had while sitting in a mandatory parenting class and being asked questions like, "What is an appropriate dinner: a) broccoli or b) ice cream?" Nevertheless, Deborah explained that she would continue to sit through those humiliating classes as long as her daughter could get help. Situations similar to Deborah's, unfortunately, are not a thing of the past and have been experienced by the majority of our collaborators. Such experiences substantiate Roberts' (1995) contentions around the criminalizing effects of motherhood, particularly for Black moms. Roberts has critically analyzed how the behavior of Black children has been used in ways that resulted in the criminalization of their mothers. Likewise, Deborah's experiences also underscore Collins (2002) notions of how motherhood can be both a joy, but may also result in Black mothers becoming "partners in their own oppression" (p. 191).

Another mother, Tanya, who is 35, similar to Deborah, detailed how the police and other state actors treated her when she sought assistance while caring for her child in crisis:

> My daughter started running away when she was 13–not understanding the situation, I used to call the police. The way they used to [deal] with me as a grown-ass adult. They used to deal with me like, even when they knew my age, they used to [deal] with me like I was still a teenager. You don't know–when I would call the police when my daughter ran away, I used to get told to shut up in my own house. In my own house, I used to get told to shut up.

Both Tanya and Deborah's narratives corroborate Roberts' (1993, 2012) assertions that the criminal justice and foster care system force Black children out of homes as a means of dividing Black families and punishing Black women and Black children. Once again, even when Black mothers try to navigate toward institutions positioned to help them with their kids, they are met with condemnation as their children are further marginalized and discursively taught their mothers are unfit.

Pamela, who is 29 years old, described how her children were impacted by the Freddie Gray case and the uprising in Baltimore. Throughout the conversation, she referenced multiple times how her oldest son, who is eight years old, articulates fear for his safety due to hyper-surveillance in their community and the constant harassment he witnesses. She laments:

> I explain to my children, and I got 3 boys, so, I explained to them about what's going on and how I want them … my oldest wants to join the military, so he was like, "Ma, I don't want to be like that," I said okay, Freddie Gray wasn't a bad person, Freddie Gray was a good person, and I showed him the pictures of Freddie that they have up in the city over on the other side. They have a big mural of him on the wall.

Another one of our collaborators, Michelle, who is 27 years old, describes how she engages in collective motherwork (Collins, 1990, 2002) also known as the act of engaging "othermotherhood." We asked what she tells her child and the children around her about police brutality and the series of events following Freddie Gray's murder. Michelle has an infant son of her own, but she describes how she sees her toddler godson cowering at police. She illustrates, "I haven't talked to any children personally. My godson is 3. He's too young to comprehend it right now. But it definitely affects them, because I think it just made them scared of the police."

Our collaborators' mothering experiences are examples of the theories proposed by Roberts (1993, 2012) and Collins (1990, 2002) regarding the adverse circumstances Black mothers find themselves in when responding to crises and attempting to protect their children. Our collaborators were each women who were not under carceral control; however, they were treated as suspects of the crime of mothering while Black. They identified the ways in which their mothering is scrutinized and supervised by the police and the child welfare system. Our collaborators' stories demonstrate the consequences of unwarranted hyper-supervision that fails to address the root cause of the crises; i.e., the need for trauma services for children in mental health crises. Therefore, the narratives from our collaborators portray the inadequacy of treating the trauma of Black children with criminal justice modalities rather than therapeutic trauma-centered crisis intervention. Moreover, the condemnation of their mothers (as they try to get their children help) show an institutional continuance in the denial of Black motherhood—and in the case of this sample, the mistreatment of children may be due to being born from Black mothers.

Black Women's Mental Health and Resilience

The demise of Black motherhood initiated by the system is a direct threat to the mental health of Black women. Black motherhood is a tool of resistance against the system and in spite of the system. Black women have been the catalyst of the essence of what a mother is and should be. Yet, the system consistently deems Black mothers as "unfit." However, Black women have historically proven to be resilient, particularly in their mothering, as they have been required to find ways to care for their own mental health while prioritizing the safety and health of their children and families (Collins, 2002).

Our collaborators shared various ways to survive when their motherhood is under attack. We found that our collaborators' methods of self-care are similar to those of women found in existing literature (Evans et al., 2017). Our collaborators shared that they regularly rely on faith-based support and artistic expression to maintain self-motivation and inner peace as they navigate the complexities of mothering and existing under oppressive methods of control. Deborah was required to do parenting classes after she sought help for her daughter's mental health struggles after her grandfather was murdered by police. Deborah's family was dismantled, and she still maintained positivity and resilience. She credited her resilience to her reliance on religion and spirituality, and she found artistic expression through singing. Deborah explained how she loves to sing, as singing psychologically liberates her from her ongoing battles with the system. All of our collaborators expressed religion was their main way to hold on to hope in times of angst regarding their families. For many of our collaborators, religion became an outlet in the absence of help from other state-sponsored sources.

Collins (2002) articulated that transcendence during periods of socialization for survival is a critical tool of encouragement that Black mothers use to push their children to be better than themselves and the manufactured negative odds in which they live. They deploy transcendence by vigorously educating their children about the intersecting oppressions they face and preparing them for success far away from their current positionality. In this spirit, we asked our collaborators what advice they would give to youth to avoid discrimination from police and the annals of living in Baltimore. The most consistent response from our collaborators was for the youth to obtain higher education. Janet, Deborah, Michelle, and Pam expressed that education is a way that youth can resist becoming a part of the system. Michelle described her daily fear of living within the conditions of hyper-surveillance in Baltimore. Michelle, a student, expressed that obtaining an education would help her to get out of Baltimore, and to ultimately avoid situations where she would be vulnerable to police violence. Other collaborators echoed Michelle's sentiments. Deborah declared, "Stay in school, get an education because the only way you can beat them is with knowledge now." Janet suggested, "I would also say to them get an education ... get a job, so you can call your own shots."

Thus, our collaborators shared what they felt has helped avoid interactions with police. Despite their efforts to avoid police violence, they have been unsuccessful most of the time. Each of their lives have been impacted, in some way, by state violence and control. They each described how either the threat of state violence, witnessing state violence, or experiencing state violence themselves has had a lasting impact on their lives. Our collaborators conveyed how their collective experiences have required them to persevere. Their resilience demonstrates the ways in which mechanisms of control have evolved and how the resilience of Black women has been inherited generationally. It should be noted, however, that this perseverance should not be read as a complete positive. Collins (2002) lamented how many outside the experience of Black womanhood conceptualizes their perseverance as strong and independent—yet inherent within this display of tenacity is the build-up of stress and other kinds of unhealthy triggers that are rendered virtually invisible. Thus, because Black women usher forward in the face of tremendous pressure, the absence of physical abnormality does not negate the presence of pain and sickness. For many collaborators, the pain was evident in their presence, voices, and stories, but acquiescing pain onto the bodies of Black women is old as slavery (Davis, 1983). Therefore, in the great American consciousness, the women in this study are experiencing a generational ritual.

DISCUSSION

Our collaborators shared a variety of personal encounters with police and state actors that have significantly impacted their lives and the lives of their children, which resulted in physical and psychological harm. Consistent with the concept of intersectionality described by Crenshaw (1991) and Potter (2015), our collaborators' narratives present significant implications for the study of state violence, Black motherhood, and reproductive justice that are incomparable to women of other races. In this section, we dissect our primary findings, some limitations of our study, and how our findings may guide future research, activism, and praxis.

Intersectionality, Reproductive Justice, and the Risk of Mothering While Black

The stories our collaborators shared affirm that being Black, a woman, and of lower socio-economic status implicates the heightened risk of being a mother. Our study illustrates that the risk of mothering for Black women presents an unparalleled reproductive justice issue that women of other races may not experience in the same manner because of the reality of intersectionality. Although research on reproductive justice has focused mostly on issues relative to accessibility of equal reproductive health services, sexual health and education, and contraception, our collaborators' experiences call for an expansion of reproductive justice research, aligned with the activism of groups such as SisterSong. Deborah and Tanya each indicate how Black women will constantly put themselves at risk of loss and trauma by reaching out for help, despite being denied multiple times. Consistent with Roberts' (1993, 1997, 1999, 2003, 2012) description of the state stripping Black women of their motherhood, especially when being criminalized while reaching out for help during crises. Therefore, we conclude that because of Black women's social location at the intersection of race-, gender-, and class-based oppression, they face reproductive justice threats beyond issues surrounding conception and access to reproductive health services. As a result, Black children are also constantly at risk of being traumatized or taken from their homes by simply existing as a Black child (and child of a Black mother) under hyper-surveillance. Thus, the trauma associated with the inability of Black mothers to safely mother their children presents a generational legacy of trauma. Our findings present a framework in which to conceptualize the unprecedented reproductive justice threats unique to Black women and how state violence controls several aspects of their lives.

Trauma, Resistance, and Creative Survival

The effects of the trauma our collaborators detail mirrors narratives of women in existing literature who have reported physical and sexual abuse (Potter, 2006). In addition, the constant state of paranoia from police surveillance mirrors the descriptions of Black women on parole and probation (Gurusami, 2019). Further, similar to Black men, Black women are presumed criminals by skin color and by association, and their interactions with police in their own communities have a similar dehumanizing and traumatic effect as the experiences of incarcerated Black women. Our collaborators describe the lived realities of surviving open-air prisons.

Consistent with CRT and BFC perspectives, the findings in this study suggest that the system inherently dehumanizes Black women and views them as animalistic. While our collaborators consistently expressed yielding help from the police turned into a degrading experience, they still repeated these acts out of desperation. Thus, our collaborators had no other known resources from which to seek help for their children, and in an effort to protect their offspring, they risked the consequences they would face by the police. Our collaborators in the study demonstrate both subconscious and conscious approaches to motherhood as resistance against hyper-surveillance and police terror and violence, as many describe instances of the integrity of their motherhood challenged by police and state actors. In addition, many suggest that education can be a vehicle to escape the communities ridden with police violence. Our collaborators also describe the reliance on religion, faith and spirituality to carry them through this turmoil exacerbated by the police. They also submerge themselves in the arts, such as music, which is utilized as a creative and emotional outlet to heal from the trauma they described.

It is recognized that the most effective method to address this research query was qualitatively, as state violence against Black women is typically unreported; therefore, it may be undetected via other methodologies. Some limitations to the study are noted as the absence of gender-specific questions and the sample size. Asking gender-specific questions particularly about how the current climate affects their mothering and their children may have elicited more detailed responses.

However, gendered implications were highlighted within our collaborator's responses. In addition, the narratives derived from a study that included men and women; therefore, the methodological approach served as a buffer to control this limitation. Lastly, although researchers typically value a larger sample size for generalizability of their findings, the purpose of this study is to explore the phenomenon of police violence and the subsequent community uprising in Baltimore. Nevertheless, the findings are consistent with and add to the body of knowledge on this topic. Future research should add to this body of knowledge to fill gaps in the understanding of Black women's perceptions and direct and vicarious traumatic experiences with police and other state actors.

CONCLUSION

Thus, the findings in this study underscore the importance of highlighting the narratives of Black women as it pertains to violence perpetuated by the police. Similarly to Black men in low-income neighborhoods, Black women are submerged in over-policed communities too. Therefore, future research cannot be complicit in perpetuating the myth of Black male exceptionalism. Black women also bear the brunt of protecting their children from the police and advocating for others around them. This is especially evident in the protests following the Freddie Gray murder in Baltimore. Vicarious and personal traumatic experiences with the police have produced a recurring pathology of broken homes and daily terror that fall on the backs of our collaborators in this study (Black women).

We found that the most imminent reproductive justice threat facing Black women in our study is the risk of mothering while Black. Black women, who live in highly policed communities are at a significant risk of physical and psychological danger because of the punitive culture of policing in cities like Baltimore. The significance of this component of reproductive justice is underscored in the stories shared by our collaborators and should be highlighted in feminist academic discourse along with other important elements of reproductive justice. If future research can incorporate the many theoretical frameworks mentioned in this study, the lived experiences of Black women and mothers can finally be known and appreciated—the future desperately depends on this rallying call. Until a more equitable society is realized, Black women will still find various methods to resist, heal, and support one another, their communities, and themselves, but at what cost to themselves and future generations of Black women and girls?

REFERENCES

Alexander, M. (2011). *The new Jim Crow: Mass incarceration in the age of colorblindness*. New Press.

Anderson, E. (1999). *Code of the street: Decency, violence, and the moral life of the inner city*. Norton & Company.

Bell, D. A. (1980). *Brown v. Board of Education* and the interest convergence dilemma. *Harvard Law Review, 93*(3), 518–533.

Bell, D. A. (1995). Who's afraid of critical race theory? *University of Illinois Law Review, 1995*(4), 893–891.

Bhattacharya, K. (2017). *Fundamentals of qualitative research: A practical guide*. Routledge.

Bloom, B., Chesney-Lind, M., & Owen, B. (1994). *Women in California prisons: Hidden victims of the war on drugs*. Center on Juvenile and Criminal Justice.

Brown, M., Ray, R., Summers, E., & Fraistat, N. (2017). #SayHerName: A case study of intersectional social media activism. *Ethnic and Racial Studies, 40*(11), 1831–1846. https://doi.org/10.1080/01419870.2017.1334934

Brunson, R. (2007). "Police don't like Black people": African-American young men's accumulated police experiences. *Criminology & Public Policy, 6*(1), 71–102. https://doi.org/10.1111/j.1745-9133.2007.00423.x

Butler, P. (2013). Black male exceptionalism? The problems and potential of black male focused interventions. *Du Bois Review: Social Science Research on Race, 10*(2), 485–511.

Clark, C., Ryan, L., Kawachi, I., Canner, M. J., Berkman, L., & Wright, R. J. (2008). Witnessing community violence in residential neighborhoods: A mental health hazard for urban women. *Journal of Urban Health, 85*(1), 22–38.

Collins, P. H. (1990). *Black feminist thought: Knowledge, consciousness, and the politics of empowerment*. Unwin Hyman.

Collins, P. H. (2002). *Black feminist thought: Knowledge, consciousness, and the politics of empowerment* (2nd ed.) Routledge.

Crenshaw, K. (1989). Demarginalizing the intersection of race and sex: A black feminist critique of antidiscrimination doctrine, feminist theory and antiracist politics. *University of Chicago Legal Forum*, *1989*(1), 139–167.

Crenshaw, K. (1991). Mapping the margins: Intersectionality, identity, politics, and violence against women of color. *Stanford Law Review*, *43*(6), 1241–1299. https://doi.org/10.2307/1229039

Crenshaw, K., Gotanda, N., Peller, G., & Thomas, K. (1996). *Critical race theory: The key writings that formed the movement*. The New Press.

Crenshaw, K., Ocen, P., & Nanda, J. (2015). Black girls matter: Pushed out, overpoliced and unprotected. *African American Policy Forum*.

Davis, A. Y. (1983). *Women, race, and class*. Vintage Books.

Du Bois, W. E. B. (1920). *Dark water: Voices from within the veil*. Harcourt Brace.

Evans, S. Y., Bell, K., Burton, N. K., & Blount, L. G. (2017). *Black women's mental health: Balancing strength and vulnerability*. State University of New York Press.

Everett, J. E., Hall, C., & Hamilton-Mason, J. (2010). Everyday conflict and daily stressors: Coping responses of Black women. *Affilia*, *25*(1), 30–42. https://doi.org/10.1177/0886109909354983

Gabbidon, S. L., Higgins, G. E., & Potter, H. (2011). Race, gender, and the perception of recently experiencing unfair treatment by the police: Exploratory results from an all Black sample. *Criminal Justice Review*, *36*(1), 5–21.

Gabbidon, S. L., & Peterson, S. A. (2006). Living while Black: A state-level analysis of the influence of select social stressors on the quality of life among Black Americans. *Journal of Black Studies*, *37*(1), 83–102.

Gurusami, S. (2019). Motherwork under the state: The maternal labor of formerly incarcerated Black women. *Social Problems*, *66*(1), 128–143.

Hill, M. L. (2018). "Thank you, Black Twitter": State violence, digital counterpolitics, and pedagogies of resistance. *Urban Education*, *53*(2), 286–302.

Jacobs, M. S. (2017). The violent state: Black women's invisible struggle against police violence. *William & Mary Journal of the Law*, *24*(039), 39–100.

Jacobs, J. (2019). Judge rescinds $38 million award to family of Maryland woman shot by police. *The New York Times*. https://www.nytimes.com/2019/02/16/us/korryn-gaines-shooting-verdict.html

James, J. (1996). *Resisting state violence: Radicalism, gender, and race in the U.S. culture*. University of Minnesota Press.

Jenkins, E. J. (2002). Black women and community violence: Trauma, grief, and coping. *Women & Therapy*, *25*(3-4), 29–44. https://doi.org/10.1300/J015v25n03_03

Jones, J. (1985). *Labor of love, labor of sorrow: Black women, work, and the family from slavery to the present*. Basic Books.

Jones-Rogers, S. E. (2019). *They were her property: White women as slave owners in the American South*. Yale University Press.

Jones, L. V., & Guy-Sheftall, B. (2015). Conquering the Black girl blues. *Social Work*, *60*(4), 343–350. https://doi.org/10.1093/sw/swv032

Jones, C. A., & Seabrook, R. L. (2017). The New Jane Crow: Mass incarceration and the denied maternity of Black women. *Sociology of Crime, Law & Deviance*, *22*, 135–154.

McMurty-Chubb, T. A. (2016). #SayHerName #BlackWomensLivesMatter: State violence in policing the Black female body. *Mercer Law Review*, *67*(3), 651–705.

Mitchell, M. B., & Davis, J. B. (2019). Formerly incarcerated Black mothers matter too: Resisting social constructions of motherhood. *The Prison Journal*, *99*(4), 420–417. https://doi.org/10.1177/0032885519852079

Moulds, E. M. (1978). Chivalry and paternalism: Disparities of treatment in the criminal justice system. *The Western Political Quarterly*, *31*(3), 416–430.

Mullings, L. (1997). *On our own terms: Race, class, and gender in the lives of African-American women*. Routledge.

Neal-Barnett, A. M., & Crowther, J. H. (2000). To be female, middle class, anxious, and Black. *Psychology of Women Quarterly*, *24*(2), 129–136. https://doi.org/10.1111/j.1471-6402.2000.tb00193.x

Paltrow, L. M. (2012). *Roe v Wade* and the New Jane Crow: reproductive rights in the age of mass incarceration. *American Journal of Public Health*, *103*(1), 17–21.

Potter, H. (2007). Battered Black women's use of religious services and spirituality for assistance in leaving abusive relationships. *Violence against Women*, *13*(3), 262–284. https://doi.org/10.1177/1077801206297438

Potter, H. (2006). An argument for Black Feminist Criminology: Understanding African American women's experiences with intimate partner abuse using an integrated approach. *Feminist Criminology*, *1*(2), 106–124.

Potter, H. (2013). Intersectional criminology: Interrogating identity and power in criminological research and theory. *Critical Criminology*, *21*(3), 305–318. https://doi.org/10.1007/s10612-013-9203-6

Potter, H. A. (2015). *Intersectionality and criminology: disrupting and revolutionizing studies of crime*. Routledge.
Rios, V. M. (2011). *Punished: Policing the lives of Black and Latino boys*. New York University Press.
Ritchie, B. E. (1996). *Compelled to crime: The gender entrapment of battered Black women*. Routledge.
Roberts, D. E. (1993). Racism and patriarchy in the meaning of motherhood. *Faculty Scholarship*. Paper 595.
Roberts, D. E. (1995). Motherhood and crime. *Social Text*, *42*, 99–123. https://doi.org/10.2307/466666
Roberts, D. E. (1997). *Killing the black body: Race, reproduction, and the meaning of liberty*. Pantheon.
Roberts, D. E. (1999). Welfare's ban on poor motherhood. In G. Mink (Ed.), *Whose welfare?* Cornell University Press.
Roberts, D. E. (2003). *Shattered bonds: The color of child welfare*. Basic Civitas Books.
Roberts, D. E. (2012). Prison, foster care, and the systemic punishment of Black mothers. *University of California Los Angeles Review*, *59*, 1474–1499.
Russell-Brown, K. (2004). *Underground codes: Race, crime and related fires*. New York University Press.
Schuh, J., Jones, S., & Harper, S. (2011). *Student services: A handbook for the profession*. Jossey-Bass.
Sharpe-Levine, J. (2019, February 1). *Intersectionality matters with Kimberle Crenshaw* [Audio podcast]. http://aapf.org/ep1-korryn-gaines
Shorter-Gooden, K. (2004). Multiple resistance strategies: How African American women cope with racism and sexism. *Journal of Black Psychology*, *30*(3), 406–425. https://doi.org/10.1177/0095798404266050
SisterSong. (2020). *SisterSong*. Retrieved from Women of Color Reproductive Justice Collective: https://www.sistersong.net/reproductive-justice
Spohn, C., & Beichner, D. (2000). Is preferential treatment of female offenders a thing of the past? A multisite study of gender, race, and imprisonment. *Criminal Justice Policy Review*, *11*(2), 149–184. https://doi.org/10.1177/0887403400011002004
St. Vil, N. M., Bushra, S., Nwokolo, V., Alexander, K. A., & Campbell, J. C. (2017). A qualitative study of survival strategies used by low-income Black women who experience intimate partner violence. *Social Work*, *62*(1), 63–76.
Steffensmeier, D., & Demuth, S. (2006). Does gender modify the effects of race-ethnicity on criminal sanctioning? Sentences for male and female White, Black and Hispanic defendants. *Journal of Quantitative Criminology*, *22*(3), 241–261.
United States Census Bureau. (2018). *Quick facts: Baltimore city, Maryland, United States*. https://www.census.gov/quickfacts/fact/table/baltimorecitymaryland,US/PST045218
United States Department of Justice (DOJ). (2016). *Investigation of the Baltimore City Policy Department*. https://www.justice.gov/opa/pr/justicedepartmentannounces-findings-investigation-baltimore-police-department
Young, V. D. (2001). All the women in the Maryland penitentiary: 1812–1869. *The Prison Journal*, *81*(1), 113–132.
Zucker, A. N. (2014). Reproductive justice: More than choice. *Analysis of Social Issues & Public Policy*, *14*(1), 210–213.

Discourses of Good Motherhood and the Policing of Young Parenthood

Amber-Lee Varadi, Rebecca Raby, and Christine Tardif-Williams

ABSTRACT
Within a neoliberal context, youth pregnancy continues to be socially recognized as an individualized mistake, influencing young mothers by shaping and constraining their actions and lifestyle choices. Utilizing a Foucauldian and poststructural feminist lens, and drawing on interviews with 11 young mothers, this research examines how, where, and why young mothers experience forms of policing. Participants conceptualized "good" motherhood through two qualities—"being there" and "taking care of herself too"—which simultaneously reproduce and resist hegemonic discourses related to normative mothering and neoliberalism. Findings also reveal how real and perceived instances of judgement resulted in young mothers' policing and/or self-policing.

INTRODUCTION

Today, youth pregnancy is frequently positioned as a tragedy, a mistake, and a "wrong" choice resulting from "careless" behavior. Various "experts," from policy makers to child care professionals, seek the "meaning" of youth pregnancy and attempt to predict the consequences of this "phenomenon" (Kelly, 2000). Consequently, young mothers become normatively recognized through knowledges which construct them as social problems linked to (and perpetuating) poverty, familial dysfunction, the breakdown of the heterosexual, nuclear family, "traditional" high school education, and "proper" childrearing (Cense & Ganzevoort, 2019; Kelly, 1998, 2000; Lesko, 1995). While (mis)informing a public consciousness on the presumed meaning and consequences of young motherhood, such discourses also work to regulate young mothers through the policing that is carried out by family, friends, and strangers around them, and through self-policing, an act that follows the internalization of outside judgement and a young mother's embeddedness in the discursive context of young motherhood (Luttrell, 2003). Within this context, our research utilizes a Foucauldian and poststructural feminist lens to examine the narratives of 11 young mothers to address the following questions: (1) how, if at all, do young mothers experience forms of policing; (2) where do these forms of policing take place when they do; and (3) why do these forms of policing take place when they do? We begin by considering the discourses which influence current understandings of young motherhood and locate these problematic understandings within today's neoliberal and putatively postfeminist context. We then describe our methods and methodology before discussing our findings, which are divided into three sections. First, we illustrate how existing discourses of "good" motherhood and neoliberal citizenship contribute to young mothers' lack of resources while also informing existing programs attempting to provide this population with support. Second, we reflect on the participants' conceptualizations of "good" motherhood—"being there" and "taking care of herself too." We show how these qualities simultaneously reproduce and resist hegemonic discourses related to normative mothering within contemporary neoliberalism. Third, we consider how both real and perceived instances of negative and positive judgement resulted in young mothers' policing and/or self-policing, which influenced their behaviors, choices, and self-beliefs as a result. We conceptualize judgement as both a form and cause of policing, as judgement from others held a regulatory function that policed young mothers and, consequently, became internalized by young mothers, leading to their own self-policing. The young mothers did not always need external judgement to self-police, however. Self-policing is also linked to a young mother's own embeddedness in the discursive context of young motherhood.

THE CONTRADICTIONS OF YOUNG MOTHERHOOD

Recognizing the various and nuanced discourses of young motherhood and their effects is crucial for current understandings of young motherhood, especially in a context where many firmly believe that we are in a postfeminist and postracial age which trivializes and denies the relevance of gender, class, and race through dominant ideas of individualism, meritocracy, and neoliberalism. Despite this context, existing literature focusing on young motherhood demonstrates how systems of inequality continue to influence and govern the lives of young mothers.

Today's understanding of youth is ambiguous, as it does not have a definite age range nor a uniform social status (Tyyskä, 2014). While ambiguous, youth can best be understood as the age period between childhood and adulthood. As the youth category stands between these two binaries, "young people are expected, and allowed, to act in particular ways and engage in particular experiences as they move toward adulthood and adult responsibilities" (Prettyman, 2005, p. 155). Consequently, youth are assumed to have achieved a certain level of maturity, knowledge, and responsibility while simultaneously still requiring more development before reaching adulthood.

Research by Sukarieh and Tannock (2011) highlights how the youth category has expanded in recent years "both horizontally, in terms of the range of people and practices it encompasses, and vertically, in terms of the chronological age range to which it is commonly understood to refer" (p. 682–683), making it difficult, if not impossible, to decide who is considered a child or an adult. Thus, the extension of the youth category has included children within its classification, pulling them away from childhood protections and assuming an independence they do not yet have. Further, vague notions of who qualifies as a youth in need of support, paired with the neoliberal discourses of independence, meritocracy, and personal responsibility, make it possible for many needed social supports to be deemed unnecessary and excessive (Fraser & Gordon, 1994; Raby, 2012; Sukarieh & Tannock, 2011). At the same time, youth are simultaneously understood as incapable and in need of "support," often in the form of surveillance and control. With merging childhood and youth categories, discourses of childhood have permeated into discourses of youth and have consequently influenced understandings which frame both children and youth as "at-risk" populations, justifying the public assessment and judgement of youth's behavior and leisure-based activities (Harlan, 2016; Sukarieh & Tannock, 2011; Tsaliki, 2015). Through this focus, acts of governance are promoted as necessary steps to ensure today's youth develop in a "positive" and "healthy" manner (Sukarieh & Tannock, 2011).

This policing intensifies for young mothers, whose decisions are often considered a reflection of their morality. Research reveals that young motherhood provokes judgement of a young woman's moral character and her ability to make "good" choices (Gregson, 2009; Kelly, 1998, 2000; Lesko, 1995; Luttrell, 2003; Pillow, 2006). This hyper focus on a young mother's "choice" isolates her from the social conditions, attitudes, people, and systems surrounding her (Greyson et al., 2019; Kelly, 1998; Spear, 2004; Wigginton & Lee, 2013). Research by Wigginton and Lee (2013) demonstrates how this contemporary hyper focus on choice and personal responsibility heightens the policing pregnant women experience. They found that women who continued their existing smoking habits during their recent pregnancies felt embarrassment, guilt, and shame for not adapting to the role of the "good" mother who is self-sacrificing and aware of any possible risk that could harm the fetus (2013). In this example, an individual's choices serve as an indicator of their "good" or "bad" character as they "are situated in the neoliberal assumption that all individuals have equal control over their behaviors, regardless of social, cultural and economic factors" (p. 467).

Within hegemonic, middle-class ideologies, pregnancy continues to be constructed as something no young woman would ever want. Geronimus (2003) examines how, for European Americans, promoting "the social control message that teenage childbearing has disastrous consequences" (p. 882) to their children is an adaptive practice, as these families have access to (and may consequently "lose") a wide range of supports contributing to their well-being. For African American families, however, these supports are unavailable or not as easily accessible (2003). Moreover, Kelly (1998) suggests that young motherhood may be a good choice for young women under certain economic circumstances and restrictions. Indeed, middle-class pathways to a "good" and "successful" adulthood—attending postsecondary education, gaining relevant work experience, taking part in extra-curricular activities, and so on—are not available to all people, let alone all women (Besen-Cassino, 2018; Edin & Kefalas, 2005; Geronimus, 2003; Kelly, 1998; SmithBattle, 2006, 2007). Research by SmithBattle (2006, 2007) reveals that while middle-class youth may view pregnancy as an event that could compromise future educational or career goals, economically disadvantaged young women who are not offered the same opportunities view motherhood as meaningful, providing them with a sense of competence and satisfaction that their present life circumstances may not have offered them (Edin & Kefalas, 2005; SmithBattle, 2006, 2007).

Research informed by the narratives and experiences of young mothers demonstrates that these young women are aware of the stereotypes that inform contemporary Western consciousness (Ellis-Sloan, 2014; Greyson et al., 2019; Kirkman et al., 2001; Prettyman, 2005). Such studies reveal that the family, friends, and strangers surrounding young mothers apply age-based assumptions to these women (Kirkman et al., 2001); that they are expected to minimize the joy of motherhood and childrearing, and represent themselves as transforming individuals on the path to redemption (Barcelos, 2014; Barcelos & Gubrium, 2014; Kelly, 2000; Prettyman, 2005); and that young mothers' are frustrated with stereotypes and discourses surrounding their youthfulness. Studies also indicate that young mothers participate in a number of activities to navigate harmful assumptions, such as providing their children with new clothing, toys, and accessories (Gregson, 2009), thus participating in consumer culture to signify "respectability" (Greyson et al., 2019); some push themselves to become better students (SmithBattle, 2006, 2007; Watson & Vogel, 2017); and others reorganize their priorities in anticipation of motherhood and quit bad habits and negative influences (SmithBattle, 2006, 2007). As well, many young mothers remind themselves that the struggles they face in their parenting are not a consequence of their youth but an experience that any mother can face and learn from (Ellis-Sloan, 2014; Kirkman et al., 2001). Importantly, the lived realities of young mothers demonstrate the significant impact positive social supports can have on these women's lives. Schools that provide daycare allow young mothers to attend school as their children are cared for in a safe environment. However, many of these schools have strict age limits regarding which children can enroll in daycare and have been found to lack a rigorous curriculum (SmithBattle, 2006; Watson & Vogel, 2017).

THEORIZING THE POLICING OF YOUNG MOTHERHOOD WITHIN A NEOLIBERAL AND POSTFEMINIST DISCURSIVE CONTEXT

Contemporary neoliberalism has actively fueled and maintained the flows of power and knowledge that uphold current systemic and institutional inequalities. Shifting responsibility from governments to individuals, neoliberalism has largely eroded once existing social safety nets as the onus of social and personal well-being is placed on individual citizens and their "earned" resources, rather than achieved or maintained with the support of public services (Côté, 2014; Daniel, 2014). By constructing individuals as autonomous "entrepreneurs" with unencumbered choices, neoliberalism depoliticizes structural inequalities, consequently fueling discourses of postracialism and postfeminism (Brown, 2006; Kelly, 1998). Following this understanding of neoliberalism, Pomerantz et al. (2013) state that this hegemonic form of citizenship implies that society has reached a postfeminist state. This postfeminist discourse asserts the idea that women can do, and have, anything so long as they work hard for it—a notion that clearly echoes the fundamentals of neoliberalism and neglects to recognize the relevance of structural inequalities, including those linked to gender, class, and race (Brown, 2006; Ringrose, 2006; Pomerantz et al., 2013). As feminism's political goals are understood as excessive in a supposedly equal society, women as a monolithic entity are expected to bask in their equality and liberation despite ongoing symptoms of sexism and gender discrimination. Within this context, we examine how resulting discourses stemming from postfeminism and responsibilized neoliberal citizenship police the lives of young mothers, a population who have seemingly diverged from current discursive expectations.

In order to critically and meaningfully examine the disciplinary discourses of young mothers, we draw on Foucault's (1977/1995, 1978) theory of discourse as well as his notion of disciplinary power to inform our definition of policing. This Foucauldian theorizing demonstrates how normative discourses possess productive and regulatory functions that shape and constrain the behaviors, actions, subjectivities, and lifestyle choices of young mothers. With this Foucauldian perspective, we also utilize a poststructural feminist lens and will discuss its application below.

This research utilizes the term *policing* to extend beyond the police and to thus encapsulate "*any activity that is expressly designed and intended to establish and maintain (or enforce) a defined order within a community*" (Hermer et al., 2012, p. 23). This term will be informed by Foucault's (1991, 1977/1995) notion of disciplinary power to underscore the regulatory and controlling qualities the act of policing entails, whether this policing is performed by outside forces or through self-policing. Through explicit and implicit norms produced discursively, alongside panoptic forms of surveillance, individuals are both regulated and regulate each other in an attempt to preserve a particular social order which serves particular interests (2012).

Noticing and analyzing the forms of policing directed toward young mothers illustrates manifestations of discrimination to consider who benefits from the maintenance of particular discourses that perpetuate the marginalization of women, youth, and young mothers. Further, analyzing the forms of self-policing that young mothers participate reveals how they resist and reproduce discourses of "good" motherhood and "good" neoliberal citizenship through actions that do or do not maintain a "defined order" (Hermer et al., 2012). The laws and social norms promoted and reproduced through the state, schools and agencies, the family, and media create visible forms of governance that young mothers may feel pressured to follow (Barcelos, 2014). While self-policing is done on the individual level, it is thus influenced by the structures and sociocultural forces surrounding the individual, leaving people pressured to conform to specific identities that may be restricting or contradictory (Ussher, 2006). The disciplinary power fueling this form of policing is "connected with morality" (Foucault, 1991, p. 91) and generates feelings of shame when individuals do not comply with the hegemonic discourses applied to them if they do not have access to counter-discourses (Bartky, 1988). These feelings of shame may intensify for young mothers due to discourses on youth, women, and female sexuality, which position these women as "immoral" for their youthfulness and related "irresponsible" sexuality (Kelly, 2000; Lesko, 1995).

We also draw on poststructural feminism, a theoretical perspective that expands on a Foucauldian perspective in order to directly focus on gendered and other inequalities. Poststructural feminism is thus critical of dominant knowledge production, organization, and maintenance, and works to understand how intersections of gender, race, class, sexuality, ethnicity, ability, and migration status are subordinated by locating subtle or masked relations of power (McNay, 1992; Pomerantz, 2008; Weedon, 1987). Young mothers are often understood as a homogenous entity and have come to symbolize a plethora of contemporary issues. As a group of women who are too often framed as irresponsible and making bad choices, today's young mothers are positioned as representing the loss of (feminine) morality and are deemed an unfair drain on scarce government recourses, making them a threat to both the family and the nation as a whole (Barcelos, 2014; Kelly, 2000; Lesko, 1995; Pillow, 2003, 2015). Through its focus on context and the organization of power relations, this theoretical perspective problematizes such a position and historical knowledges that have been shrugged off as "the way it is," moves beyond essentialist ideas about women, youth, and young mothers, and shatters a single, objective meaning for young motherhood (McNay, 1992; St. Pierre, 2000).

METHODS AND METHODOLOGY

This research emerged from a community-based research project, where we collected data for Young Parents Support Program (YPSP), a local organization that provides schooling and childcare for young parents, to evaluate the effectiveness of a mentorship program developed to support young parents and address the levels of isolation many young parents experience across the summer. We conducted semi-structured, one-on-one, qualitative interviews with 11 young mothers who were enrolled in this program. Most of the participants were interviewed at three separate time points across 2018—once before the mentorship program began, another before the school term was complete, and again at the end of summer. Of our 11 participants, nine were white while two identified as Indigenous, and most (but not all) of the young mothers were in heterosexual relationships across our interviews. Class positioning was similar across many of the participants as well, with all but one coming from more working-class backgrounds.

While many of the interview questions were designed to gain insight into the participants' personal lives, several of the open-ended questions directly addressed participants' ideas about "good" motherhood and their experiences of judgement and praise. Our analysis in this paper focuses on the participants' responses to these topics. After an initial open-coding process that enabled us to identify themes across our data set, a critical discourse analysis (CDA) was applied to the codes that resonated with themes of "good" mothering, stigma, judgement, and praise. CDA encourages a systemic examination of "opaque" relationships between power/knowledge and discourse with a recognition that discourses both reflect and reproduce particular social structures and participate in the reproduction, maintenance, dismissal and, importantly, resistance to inequalities (Fairclough, 1993; McGregor, 2003; van Dijk, 1995). Discursive relations of power are boundless, shifting, and paradoxical, and CDA allowed us to notice which subjectivities and consequential possibilities were available to some young mothers and what conditions made those subjectivities attainable.

FINDINGS AND DISCUSSION

Our findings are organized into three sections. First, we introduce the young mothers' contexts, with a particular focus on areas where they experience a lack of support. We illustrate how existing discourses of young motherhood not only contribute to their lack of resources, but also work to inform programs attempting to provide young mothers with support and resources. Second, we discuss how the participants conceptualized "good" motherhood through two qualities: the mother "being there" for her child and "taking care of herself too." We outline how these two qualities both reproduce and resist discourses relating to normative mothering within today's ideology of intensive mothering and a neoliberal ethos promoting the responsibilization of its citizens (Baker, 2009; Elliott et al., 2015; Hays, 1996; Hermer et al., 2012). Third, we analyze the young mothers' experiences of judgement and praise, recognizing how these instances of negative and positive judgement are rooted in discourses that position older, middle-class motherhood as "normal" and "ideal" and, consequently, "good."

Context: Challenges and the Role of Discourses in Shaping Resources

The way in which young mothers are hegemonically represented and understood influences both the accessibility of the resources directed toward them and the aims of these resources. Sociocultural forces, institutional influences, and social relationships ubiquitously affect the lives of young mothers through their ability to inform the assumptions held toward this population, and consequently create narratives that young mothers must navigate (Barcelos & Gubrium, 2014). For instance, a focus on their deviant youthfulness as mothers informs how young mothers are recognized when establishing the "supports" necessary for their chances of future success. Kelly (2000) highlights the significance of these age-based discourses:

> Whether teen mothers are cast as unloved victims or as rebellious threats, by virtue of their age, they are seen as children who must be 'helped' by adults. Defining teen mothers as by that very fact 'immature' inevitably shapes the programs and policies established to address their needs; thus, supervision, monitoring, and surveillance become the resulting watchwords of such programs. (p. 35)

Influenced by these various discourses, if young mothers are hegemonically understood as irresponsible, blemished, and in need of control, supports are often about surveillance, when more practical support is needed. For instance, young mothers' current and future well-being are likely to benefit from educational and child care supports, flexibility within their work schedules as well as a living wage, and emotional supports. The limited existing practical supports create barriers for this population (SmithBattle, 2006). The influence of contemporary neoliberalism encourages and expects young mothers to become self-reliant with little to no acknowledgement of structural constraints, such as sexism and the stigma against young motherhood (Lesko, 1995). An effect of these problematic discourses is an absence of sufficient supports necessary for young mothers' well-being. Three supports that were deemed as necessary but not easily available or inaccessible were identified.

Needed Supports

First, there was a clear need for greater mental health support, as many of the young mothers experienced different mental health struggles, including depression and postpartum depression, anxiety and social anxiety, posttraumatic stress disorder, obsessive compulsive disorder, borderline personality disorder, bipolar disorder, and bulimia. Raven, a 22-year-old student and mother of her three-year-old daughter, Lucy, illustrates the prevalence of mental health struggles across her classmates while discussing the climate of the YPSP classroom: "we've all pretty much been through things and we all pretty much have depression and stuff, so some people don't think before they speak and they kind of hit people's triggers." While participants understood their mental health struggles as one of their primary challenges in their day-to-day experiences, they did not receive enough support. With no one in their life to talk to about their mental health, Monica and Selena both explained how counselling would be beneficial for their mental health, as prescription medication had not helped them in the past. Their attempts to receive counselling, however, were largely unsuccessful. Monica was dismissed by her doctor, who told her that counselling would be ineffective: "I've tried talking to my doctor and he's just like [...] 'we can put you back on antidepressants but we're not going to let you talk to anyone because that's not going to help you at this point.'" Selena explained how she used to receive counselling but had to stop due to its distance from her home and financial constraints.

Young mothers may experience a heightened vulnerability to these mental health struggles due to social disadvantages that preceded their pregnancies and, as mentioned, as a consequence of new adversities and disadvantages introduced with motherhood, especially as a young woman (SmithBattle & Freed, 2016). Research by SmithBattle and Freed (2016) similarly identifies conditions which may lead to or worsen existing mental health struggles, such as "the stress of parenting, economic hardships, intimate partner violence, and the stigma of early childbearing" (SmithBattle & Freed, 2016, p. 32). This finding suggests that the mental health struggles young mothers experience may be linked to the hegemonic discourses surrounding young motherhood and underscores the need to reveal the harms that materialize with the existence and circulation of such discourses.

Second, the young mothers also struggled with institutional barriers, specifically those relating to housing, leaving many participants needing to escape toxic family members and crowded living conditions. Some of the young mothers said that their living situation was a primary struggle in their lives, negatively influencing their mental health and creating strain in family relationships. Kikyo, for example, stated that she is "trying my hardest to get out of there" after talking about the verbal and physical abuse she faced from her relative, who she was living with, and its negative impact on her mental health and self-esteem. Young mothers' struggle to secure adequate housing is likely due to the stigma associated with young motherhood, where young mothers are understood as "welfare dependent, geographically immobile, poorly educated and with apparently limited vision," making them the "antithesis" (Arai, 2009, p. 181) of today's neoliberal agenda.

Third, programs created to support young mothers, such as YPSP, offer much needed childcare while they are in school, but many of the young mothers still needed consistent after-school care, especially for those who worked or needed to work. While a lack of childcare made work harder to access for some of the young mothers, other participants, like Monica, explained how their families' help with childcare created new stressors: "[childcare's] hard on [my mom] [...] she works overnight [...] So she's not really getting any sleep, but when I'm at work [...] I can't watch [my son], obviously, so it's one of the two of them." SmithBattle and Freed (2016) describe how support from the mothers of young mothers, while a primary and reliable source of support for many young mothers, may introduce new problems such as criticism, family conflicts, and resentment.

It is also important to draw attention to two mothers who did not indicate as much of a need for such supports. Described as a "pretty, young girl," 18-year-old Katia captured the idealized version of young motherhood: white, middle-class, well-supported by her family, and, consequently, not reliant on social support. Katia's class and alignment with certain hegemonic norms surrounding 'good' motherhood offered her a support system that benefitted her personally and systemically, affording her a sense of comfort and stability that many young mothers do not have. Jade, a 22-year-old Indigenous mother, also seemed to have more support than other participants, due to extended family networks. She said: "I can pick up the phone for anything and it's just full support." This finding overlaps with existing literature with young Indigenous mothers, which illustrates how young Indigenous mothers and their children experience high levels of support, valuation, and acceptance from their extended families and surrounding Indigenous communities (Greyson, O'Brien, & Shoveller, 2017; Kelly, 2000). However, as argued by Salmon (2007), despite positive conceptualizations of young motherhood within Indigenous communities, young Indigenous mothers are targeted and constructed as 'bad' mothers by certain 'preventative' and 'educational' Canadian polices that frame these mothers as threats to their children's health. Influenced by today's neoliberal and neocolonial context, these sites of discourse production and maintenance significantly harm the mothering experiences of young Indigenous women, and further marginalize young Indigenous mothers through intensive State and medicalized surveillance that may be largely unfamiliar to other young mothers.

The supports and lack of supports mentioned here are largely shaped by dominant discourses of youth, mothering, and young motherhood that are followed with certain consequences. A lack of mental health supports left some of the mothers feeling isolated, self-conscious, and anxious, and pushed some to a form of responsibilized self-policing, where they took matters into their own hands and relied solely on self-care behaviors to manage their mental health struggles. Some of the young mothers lived in isolation or toxic environments with family members due to a lack of support in overcoming housing barriers, and we argue that this finding reveals a concrete consequence of discourse, where negative discourses surrounding youth and young mothers influenced their opportunities for accessing housing (Arai, 2009; Lesko, 1995). Finally, a need for childcare influenced some of the young mothers' lifestyles as childcare challenges determined how they could spend their time after school and their availability for work. Through expectations of individualism and self-reliance in a postfeminist state, young mothers face, and will continue to experience, an absence of sufficient supports necessary for their well-being.

Good Mom

In addition to asking about their welfare and daily interactions with their children, we asked the young mothers: "what do you feel makes someone a good mom?" There were two common ways that most of the participants talked about "good" motherhood: the mother "being there" for her child and "taking care of herself too."

"Being There"

"Being there" as a quality of "good" motherhood came up frequently, with many of the mothers stressing its importance in their children's lives and future well-being. When asked what they believe makes someone a good mom, many of the responses touched on "being there": "[b]eing there is just a big deal. I know so many parents who are just so absent in their child's lives and they don't even realize how much it affects their kids until it's too late" (April); "you know, just being there" (Selena); "being there for your kids […] not neglecting them, that's a big one for me" (Drew). In her second interview, Drew built on this quality's description: "[b]eing there for your child, for sure. Being very supportive of them and putting all your time into them." With this description, we can begin to notice the intensive quality behind these two words: "being there," as the young mothers underscore, demands much more than the mother's presence alone. From the young mothers' answers, we learn that "being there" is about presence, support, and investing time and energy. The quality of "being there" worked as both a site of discourse reproduction and discourse resistance.

The young mothers' descriptions of "being there" demonstrate which discourses of appropriate, ideal, and "good" motherhood are active today, and resonate with Hays' (1996) focus on the ideology of intensive mothering. While Hays' research concentrates on an ideology rather than a discourse of motherhood, she considers how the ideology of intensive mothering is not natural nor inevitable but, rather, socially constructed. We utilize and apply Hays' ideology of mothering like discourse as it reveals notions of appropriate and ideal motherhood that have regulatory effects (1996). As stated by Elliott et al. (2015), intensive mothering "capture[s] the increasingly common belief that good mothers should first and foremost be caregivers and should invest great swaths of time, money, energy, and emotional labor in intensively raising children" (p. 352). Consider Selena's response to what she believes makes someone a "good" mother:

> [W]hat you put out to [your children] is how they're gonna be. So, like, you have to be positive all the time. I mean, not all the time but, like, the majority of the time because […] they'll learn that behavior and […] negative behaviors, that's learnt […] nobody is just born that way […] some people are like, 'well I gotta put myself first.' But, like, you know, your child's first […] and you have to always maintain that good and positive, you know, energy and stuff towards them.

While Selena's description of a "good" mom centers around the quality of "being there," it also introduces the demanding characteristics of this ideal of "good" motherhood. Hays (1996) argues that the emotional-, labour-, and finance-exhausting parenting promoted through intensive mothering is justified, as it is deemed necessary for the "protection and preservation" of children's "inherent goodness." As the belief that children are a product of their mothers' active, informed, and careful participation in their lives becomes more prominent, the idea that an intensively child-devoted mother is a "good" mother has become normalized as a necessary form of mothering. Mothers are thus obliged to offer their children the "best," most intensive and consistent care as they are held responsible for their children's future behaviors, characters, and life paths.

In light of Hays' arguments, we can begin to recognize how young mothers experience particular scrutiny and judgement about whether they sufficiently fulfill the ideals of intensive mothering. Selena's response demonstrates an internalization of such judgement as she questions her behaviours and self-beliefs as a 'good' mother when answering the question: "do you feel like a 'good' mom?":

> I mean, like, I do feel like a good mom but sometimes when [my daughter], like, acts out and stuff, it makes me feel like maybe I'm not doing what I'm supposed to do […] she's, ah, got a bit of an attitude. And I'm like, 'is that *me*? Did I do that?' […] So I'm, like, is it–am I not being attentive enough to her?

"Being there" assumes an idealized form of parenting, where the mother must not only physically be with her child, but provide her attention and positive emotionality as well. However, while this form of "good" mothering is demanding, typically assumed of the mother alone, and physically, mentally, and emotionally exhausting, "being there" could also be deployed by the mothers as a form of resistance. It allowed the young mothers to position and understand themselves as good mothers, illustrating their dedication to "being there" for their children, especially if they could not do so financially. Also, and reflecting findings by Kirkman et al. (2001), the participants felt that their youthfulness enabled them to succeed at "being there" in a more active and playful way compared to other, older mothers who delayed childbearing.

"Taking Care of Herself Too"

Along with "being there," many of the young mothers believed that a "good" mother ensures that she is "taking care of herself too." "Taking care of herself too" interestingly contrasts with the idea of "being there," thus illustrating the intensive, demanding, and contradictory characteristics involved in "good" motherhood. After describing the quality of "being there" in her first interview, Raven continues to discuss what she believes makes someone a "good" mom:

> And then it's also to love yourself […] because if you don't take care of yourself, you're not going to be able to take care of them. I learned that really early on because I–I completely gave up on myself when I was pregnant. And right after Lucy was born, I wouldn't do my hair, I wouldn't get dressed […] I always felt gross, and I was always mad at Lucy because I was always angry with myself […] So when I started to take care of myself and give myself baths and go out for dinner with my girlfriend–as soon as I did things for myself, I was able to come home and feel good, and be like, "I missed you. I love you."

Raven explains how taking care of oneself as a mother is not only necessary for the mother to be happy, but for the mother to thrive in her role as a parent as well. Selena similarly emphasized how beneficial taking care of oneself is in one's parenting and stressed how self-care may also model healthy habits.

These aspects of "taking care of herself too" came up frequently as participants answered questions relating to their well-being and healthy behaviors. However, some participants who were struggling with their mental health and low self-esteem expressed difficulties in finding the energy and purpose to pursue such self-care activities. As Monica reflected, "I put myself on a backburner usually." The following two sub-sections discuss how this quality of "good" motherhood reproduces and resists existing discourses surrounding young motherhood and the "good" neoliberal citizen.

"Taking care of herself too" and contemporary neoliberalism. As mothers are expected to radically adjust their lives after their pregnancies, self-care may appear as a selfish act in the mother's child-centered world. This assumption can be found in Selena's comment on "being there" mentioned above, where she says mothers should not put themselves first if they are caring for a child. However, Selena was also one of the young mothers who underscored the importance of a "good" mother's self-care, therefore demonstrating how abstract, unstable, and messy the boundaries between "good" mothering and "bad" mothering are, and where the difference between "selfish" behavior and "productive" or "necessary" behavior are unstable and vague. The various discourses on motherhood are constantly influencing and shaping how mothers practice "good" parenting, and also how they are judged.

Encouraging values of individualism and personal responsibility, today's neoliberal ethos nuances this quality of "good" mothering as it promotes responsibilization through self-care. Through the belief that individuals are in complete control of their lives, its consequences, and resulting emotions, neoliberal discourses consequently assume that individuals hold the ability to be happy and fulfilled through acts such as self-care. Charlie explains how taking care of herself is directly linked to being a "good" mother: "making sure that you are happy in your role and healthy in your role. Cuz if you're not happy being a mom, then you're not healthy and taking care of yourself. You can't take care of your child." According to Charlie, you must be happy and healthy to be a "good" mother, and these are not qualities that come without taking care of yourself as well as your child. Following this logic, a mother who is unhappy with her position as a mother is not taking care of herself. Moreover, the implication of this association is that a mother who is struggling is clearly not taking care of herself. This logic supports today's neoliberal discourse, which overlooks social inequalities by narrowing all focus to the individual. In this way, self-care is deemed accessible to all and, therefore, happiness and fulfillment are assumed to be just as achievable.

Resistance through "taking care of herself too." In moments of burnout, Raven shared how taking care of herself is necessary for her well-being: "[s]ometimes I feel like I've pushed too hard on myself and then I'm like, "I need some self-care." So I go do something dumb like take a bath or read a book." By calling these self-care activities "dumb," Raven is undermining the necessity behind these actions of self-compassion. Despite the manner in which Raven discussed self-care, she continued to participate in these activities when she needed them most, recognizing that she needs to care for herself as well as her child. Despite its failure to recognize the relevance of structural constraints and inequalities, similar to "being there," the quality of "taking care of oneself too" works to resist discourses that position young motherhood as "bad" motherhood by enabling the participants to feel that they are succeeding as good mothers. Through this quality of good motherhood, the participants can recognize the state of their mental, emotional, and physical health, and aim to take the necessary steps to improve and maintain their positive well-being. The young mothers thus successfully positioned their rather contained and affordable attempts at self-care (e.g., taking a bath, dying their hair, and "binge watch[ing] movies" with a friend) as a necessary quality to achieve "good" motherhood. Accordingly, "taking care of herself too" allows the young mothers to understand themselves as good mothers despite their youth and financial constraints, and the problematic discourses that surround young motherhood.

In summary, the two qualities of "good" motherhood identified by the young mothers—"being there" and "taking care of herself too"—work as sites of discourse maintenance and reproduction, as well as strategies of resistance. "Being there" was found to align with the ideology of intensive mothering (Hays, 1996) while also working as a form of resistance to hegemonic norms surrounding "good," older, and middle-class motherhood, allowing the young mothers to understand and position themselves as "good" mothers. "Taking care of herself too" similarly reproduced neoliberal ideals of the "good" individualized and responsibilized citizen while enabling the participants to resist discourses that position young motherhood as "bad" motherhood.

Judgement and Praise

All 11 of the young mothers in our sample experienced negative judgement. As today's "catch-all-enemies" (Kelly, 2000) through discourses that position young mothers as "lazy," "selfish," and "irresponsible," young mothers' experiences of judgement may come from family, friends, and strangers alike, and take several forms, leaving young mothers feeling much like Kikyo: "I feel like I'm being judged everywhere I go, pretty much." April elaborates on this point when asked if she ever feels judged negatively for her parenting:

> When I go out in public, I'm judged everywhere I go, *all* the time. When I tell my kids they can't buy a Kinder Egg because they don't need it, I'm judged. Like, I'm judged for everything […] every single person you will talk to from YPSP will tell you they are judged every day no matter what they're doing […] because, you know, they're doing *something* wrong in *somebody's* eyes […] If you're not doing something everybody else's way, it's a problem, basically […] And because we're young, we're dumb, and we don't know anything. Of *course*, right?

Many participants' discussions of judgement were rooted in negative discourses on youth and young mothers. The young mothers frequently mentioned receiving stares from strangers when their children were crying or having a tantrum in public spaces (e.g., grocery stores):

> Kikyo: When she's whiney and I can't get her to stop or she's just screaming, people are staring. And then I get stares sometimes because I'm also–like, I'm 22 but I look younger so people think, like, I'm just, like, some teen mom.

> Monica: And then I feel like in public I–I can't stand going anywhere in public with him cuz he has constant meltdowns and I feel judged by other people then. If we're in the middle of the store and he's screaming and crying– [I: Right. You feel like people are scrutinizing you?] Mhm.

Our analysis of these experiences suggests that the judgement and resulting insecurity and self-policing felt and practiced by these young mothers may stem from dominant discourses of young motherhood that position young mothers as unable to properly care for their children compared to older mothers, who are assumed to have put more time and effort into their childrearing abilities (Kelly, 2000). Through her description of others' judgement, where she believes that strangers assume she is "just […] some teen mom," Kikyo reveals the effect of discourse, which not only negatively categorizes and simplifies young mothers, but may result in young mothers' self-policing – a practice following the internalization of these discourses and outside judgement.

Through two experiences, Selena outlined instances where she perceived judgement from others in the form of "side-glances." In one experience, she discussed how she perceived this form of judgement when buying junk food with her partner and daughter: "[w]e get her things that she needs, her clothes, and *then* we go and get food and stuff […] and we really try hard to get healthy food but sometimes we don't so, like, that's where the side-glances come in sometimes." It can be argued that this perceived judgement overlaps with the "neglectful mother" discourse, where Selena may have been perceived as unwilling to make the "right" and "good" choices for herself and her daughter. Through another experience, she talked about how she felt judgement while shopping alone with her daughter and being perceived as a *single* young mother: "I used to get that [side-glances] when I would go to [the grocery store] […] When I would go there by myself, you know, I would get side looks, like, 'oh, where's the dad?'" The policing of young motherhood is possible when young motherhood is held as the "immoral" and "inappropriate" form of motherhood against normative motherhood, where an adult mother is in a heterosexual marriage, educated, and employed (Kelly, 2000; Kirkman et al., 2001).

Young Mothers' Engagement with and Resistance to Judgement

The young mothers' feelings of self-consciousness and worry following instances of both real and perceived judgement resulted in their self-policing as they internalized this judgement and altered their behaviors, actions, and shopping habits as a result. Judgement also resulted in several forms of resistance, and these acts of engagement and resistance will be discussed below.

Self-policing. In all three of her interviews, Raven talked about how she "dealt with" judgement through self-policing and altering her behavior to avoid future judgement. In one example, Raven talked about her experience of judgement at a grocery store where a stranger told her "[y]ou shouldn't even have your child" when she could not stop her daughter, Lucy, from crying after almost two hours and told her with frustration to "shut up." Following this experience, Raven said: "I just try to keep my cool better, especially in public because people are always watching and judging. And then when I'm at home, if I feel overwhelmed, I just walk away from it. I just let Lucy do whatever she's doing and then come back to it." In addition to "keep[ing] my cool better," Raven altered her choices and removed herself from certain locations altogether: "usually [I] just leave the store or take deep breaths, count to ten"; "if she's really crying and people are really staring […] I usually just leave." This self-policing, which Raven participated in both when she was in and out of the public eye, reveals the disciplinary and affective role judgement possesses. Here, the relevance of the metaphor of the panopticon becomes apparent: both real and perceived judgement worked to discipline the young mothers regardless of whether they were in a store or at home. The ubiquity of discourses of young motherhood creates a permanent visibility that the young mothers must navigate, where each mother "becomes to [her]self [her] own jailer" (Bartky, 1988, p. 63).

It is valuable to consider whether this instance of public beratement was related to Raven's youthfulness or class. In another example, Raven admitted that she stopped using her daughter's stroller because it "wasn't exactly, like, the nicest looking stroller. It was a second-hand stroller. So I used to feel like I was getting judged for that." Raven also stated that she stopped taking public transit while using her stroller due to the judgement she would receive while on the bus: "if I need to get groceries or anything, I'll either walk or I'll cab it." This illustrates how young mothers' assumed poverty may worsen the judgement they receive, and further influence the actions, behaviors, and choices they make due to their self-policing.

Similar to Raven, Monica's behavior was also influenced by her internalization of the judgement of others. After being asked if she feels judgement outside of the home, Monica confessed that she now avoids others' judgement by not going out with her son at all: "I try not to go anywhere with him because he has tantrums and stuff, and it embarrasses me […] If I want to go somewhere, I wait until he's not around so he doesn't have to go with me." Monica's solution to avoid judgement through her self-policing is stark, as it contributes to the isolation of her and her son. Further, this isolation may exacerbate Monica's existing mental health struggles and her understanding of herself as a "bad" mom.

Kikyo also talked about cutting herself off from talking to strangers to avoid judgement. The partial and complete isolation taken on by the young mothers in order to avoid judgement may result in a lack of opportunity to connect with their children and worsen their negative self-perceptions as "bad" mothers. The metaphor of the panopticon can be applied to these instances of self-policing, as these women have internalized the regulation resulting from the negative judgement they have experienced. Monica and Kikyo's experiences of self-policing reveal how the influence of discourse and disciplinary power "constitutes the very subjectivity of the subject" (Bartky, 1988, p. 80).

Across these examples, the judgement informed by hegemonic discourses of young motherhood possessed a disciplinary power, where the young mothers' behaviors and actions were influenced and altered, sometimes making their present realities more isolated, through limited interaction, or onerous, by walking or using money to take a taxi. Internalized judgement from others also influenced some of the participants' self-beliefs. Selena confessed that the stigma of being a young mother often undermined her positive self-talk that acknowledged the work and care she put into her parenting and negatively impacted her self-esteem:

> I'm like, 'I should be doing more […] I should be further in life right now.' Like, I'm gonna be 22 and I'm still trying to finish high school. And that's not a bad thing because I'm still trying to finish but it's–in my opinion on myself, I feel like it's bad because it's taken this long […] you know, I'm still trying to finish high school. I fricking work at [a fast-food chain]. You know, like, it's just a bunch of those things. And I just feel like I should be doing better.

Selena's self-beliefs, where she believes she "should be doing more" and "doing better," relate to the expectation of "redemption" assigned to young mothers who are pressured to "redeem" themselves through their assimilation to normative life courses (i.e., postsecondary education, full-time work, heterosexual marriage) (Barcelos, 2014; Elliott et al., 2015; Luttrell, 2003; Prettyman, 2005). Despite the fact that she was juggling her roles as a student, employee, and mother, Selena continued to feel shame for not achieving a normative life course. Selena's self-beliefs worked as a form of self-policing, where she pressured herself to achieve a "normative" identity in spite of her status as a young mother.

Recognizing and challenging unfair judgement. The young mothers engaged with and resisted judgement by recognizing and challenging its unfair nature. While some participants were indeed affected by judgement, they were simultaneously critical of it. April, for example, recognized the unfair nature of the judgement she received:

> People are so stereotypical. People think that I drink all the time. People think that I do drugs and that I'm a whore and […] all this ridiculous stuff […] I get it cuz, like, I'm 20 but at the same time […] there's a lot of people that work their asses off to be good parents at a young age […] Not everybody is a bad mom just because they're young […] And you get judged for the same things that are happening to everybody else.

April resisted self-policing by challenging judgement and recognizing its unfair nature. She emphasized the hard work that many young mothers put into their parenting while recognizing how older mothers do not experience the same hyper-critical surveillance many young mothers are familiar with.

The young mothers' abilities to internalize or challenge judgement were nuanced and often overlapping. For example, while some of the young mothers responded to judgement through self-policing, they were simultaneously critical of this judgement. While Kikyo's statements demonstrate her self-policing following public judgement, they also reveal her critical attitude toward this judgement. By recognizing how "[p]eople are just gonna talk no matter what," it can be argued that Kikyo, like April, similarly recognizes how she will experience judgement no matter the situation.

As well as recognizing and challenging unfair judgement, some participants resisted negative judgement by acknowledging their perseverance and exercising self-compassion. Drew, for example, exercised perseverance as she talked about her father: "he always told me I would never make it on my own and here I am […] He was like, 'you wouldn't last two weeks without living here.' And I lasted a long time." By recognizing where she is today, Drew attests her perseverance, something that took her beyond her father's negative expectations.

The young mothers also resisted judgement by judging other mothers. This effect did not result in their self-policing but, rather, served as a justification to continue their current, positively-framed, parenting methods. An example of this is an experience of Brad's, who recalled a day where she was playing outside with her son and was visible to two older women across the street:

> They're just looking at me, shaking their heads […] and I'm like, "what? Is this wrong?" […] These mothers are just sitting there, they look like their kids were just, like, five and eight. There's […] two kids playing with each other. And they're like, 'mom! Come do this!' And [the mothers are] like, 'no.'

Brad defended herself against negative judgement by focusing on how she was more engaged with her child than the two mothers across the road, who, according to Brad, were simply ignoring their children. Eighteen-year-old Topaz judged other mothers for "always [going] out and leaving their child" and mothers who "rely on child tax benefits, which is not good," thus reproducing judgement she may face for being a young mother. By succeeding in areas of motherhood that they suggested was lacking in other mothers, these young mothers successfully challenged negative feelings that some of the other participants faced and did not feel pressured to alter their current behaviors, actions, or choices.

Praise and Positive Judgement

Praise, while positive and often embraced by the participants, also worked as a form of policing. Praise reveals socially constructed ideas of "good" and "bad" forms of motherhood, where the former is "deserving" of this positive judgement. Praise may also work to produce certain kinds of motherhood that comply with normative discourses of middle-class, older motherhood and further reproduce negative discourses of young motherhood.

As mentioned above, the young mothers resisted negative judgement through their ability to recognize themselves as "doing a good job." However, the young mothers were not the only ones who believed they were "doing a good job." The participants frequently spoke of instances where the people around them also told them that they were "doing a good job." For instance, Drew states: "my friends and my mom, my godmother, they tell me a lot, that I'm a good mom and I'm doing a good job. And it's nice to hear." Similar comments were made by Selena, Raven, Charlie, and April. Our analysis of these comments found that the recognition of young mothers as "doing a good job," while valuable affirmation, may also insidiously work to underscore how their mothering is deviant to the norm and is consequentially a target of surveillance, critique, and policing as an "inmate" of the panopticon.

CONCLUSION

Through this research, we have looked at the various discourses which contribute to the policing of young motherhood. Using a Foucauldian and poststructural feminist perspective with the application of CDA, we found that this policing is enacted through various discourses relating to a young mother's age, gender, class, working status, and mothering. Moreover, the overlapping of these discourses, along with values of individualism and responsibilization perpetuated by a neoliberal and postfeminist ethos, creates more nuanced forms of inequality and policing, and influence areas outside of a young mother's parenting, such as the supports she does and does not receive, as a result.

Informed by the narratives of 11 young mothers, we learned how and where policing and self-policing occurred, and why particular instances of policing transpired. These findings, however, may be specific to this study and its participants, and these particularities must be acknowledged. Reflecting on their research experience with a parent support program similar to YPSP, Greyson et al. (2017) stress how recruitment within these programs may result in participant limitations, as "mothers on both the most- and least-disadvantaged ends of the spectrum… would be the least likely to be engaged with young parent services" (p. 147). It is crucial to consider how a young mother's race, class, migration status, sexuality, and ability, for example, may influence her understanding of "good" motherhood and experiences of policing, judgement, and praise, and a wider sample may have resulted in more nuanced narratives speaking to these differences.

For instance, a sample including more participants like Charlie, a 22-year-old mother in a same-sex relationship, would invite a new area of analysis that could consider how young mothers experience their queer romantic relationships. In her first interview, Charlie talked about how her new relationship with her girlfriend "is probably the most healthy relationship I've been in." In her second interview, she exclaimed how this growing relationship was a solid foundation of support in her life. As she thrives in this romantic relationship with her same-sex partner, Charlie's circumstances prompt further considerations: how are young mothers' queer romantic relationships perceived, and does a young mother's queerness invite new forms of judgement, surveillance, and policing?

Moreover, a young mother's intersecting social position will influence how she is interpreted and consequently treated (Kelly, 2000). Several Canadian studies have revealed that young Indigenous mothers' experiences of policing are pervasive in a way that is unfamiliar to those populations who have not experienced the historical violence, oppression, and marginalization of colonialism. Colonization has resulted in the perception of young Indigenous mothers as ignorant due to the delegitimizing of traditional Indigenous parenting practices and an assumed disregard to privileged "scientific," Western prenatal and parenting knowledges (Greyson et al., 2017; Kelly, 2000; Salmon, 2007). These problematic discourses have resulted in "preventative" and "educational" policies and campaigns targeting Indigenous mothers which mask ongoing symptoms of colonialism through a focus on the individual and their "choices" and further construct young Indigenous mothers as "dangerous" and "threats" to their children's well-being (Salmon, 2007). Consequentially, young Indigenous mothers may be interpreted as "bad" mothers due to their Indigeneity alone and, as demonstrated, experience ensuing negative treatment.

Through both real and perceived judgement, and also through instances of praise, findings demonstrated how young mothers were policed, for example, through side-glances and unwarranted comments from strangers. Moreover, judgement and praise resulted in some of the young mothers' self-policing. The idea of young mothers' self-policing would be valuable to take into account while conducting future research on young motherhood, especially while considering how race, class, migration status, and sexuality may influence these actions, choices, and beliefs. Future research should also consider how and where the regulatory function of discourse influences other marginalized groups across the West, such as LGBT identifying individuals, Indigenous people, migrant groups, people of color, and working-class groups. These "othered" groups may experience similar manifestations of policing through particular forms of judgement and praise, and it would be valuable to consider how these forms of negative and positive judgement are produced and maintained, and to analyze their effects.

Funding

This work was supported by the Brock University Social Justice Research Institute and the United Way Special Projects Fund.

ORCID

Rebecca Raby http://orcid.org/0000-0002-7830-2960

REFERENCES

Arai, L. (2009). What a difference a decade makes: Rethinking teenage pregnancy as a problem. *Social Policy & Society*, *8*(2), 171–183.

Baker, J. (2009). Young mothers in late modernity: Sacrifice, respectability and the transformative neo-liberal subject. *Journal of Youth Studies*, *12*(3), 275–288.

Barcelos, C. A. (2014). Producing (potentially) pregnant teen bodies: Biopower and adolescent pregnancy in the USA. *Critical Public Health*, *24*(4), 476–488.

Barcelos, C. A., & Gubrium, A. C. (2014). Reproducing stories: Strategic narratives of teen pregnancy and motherhood. *Social Problems*, *61* (3), 466–481.

Bartky, S. L. (1988). Foucault, femininity, and the modernization of patriarchal power. In I. Diamond & L. Quinby (Eds.), *Feminism & Foucault: reflections on resistance* (pp. 61–86). Northeastern University Press.

Besen-Cassino, Y. (2018). *The cost of being a girl: Working teens and the origins of the gender wage gap*. Temple University Press.

Brown, W. (2006). American nightmare: Neoliberalism, neoconservatism, and de- democratization. *Political Theory, 34*(6), 690–714. doi:10.1177/0090591706293016

Cense, M., & Ganzevoort, R. (2019). The storyscapes of teenage pregnancy. On morality, embodiment, and narrative agency. *Journal of Youth Studies, 22*(4), 568–583. doi:10.1080/13676261.2018.1526373

Côté, J., (2014). Education and the youth period. In J. Côté (Ed.), *Youth studies: Fundamental issues and debates* (pp. 79–98). Palgrave.

Daniel, C. (2014). "Taming the media monster": Teen pregnancy and the neoliberal safety (inter)net. *Signs: Journal of Women in Culture and Society, 39*(4), 973–998.

Edin, K., & Kefalas, M. (2005). *Promises I can keep: Why poor women put motherhood before marriage*. University of California Press.

Elliott, S., Powell, R., & Brenton, J. (2015). Being a good mom: Low-income, black single mothers negotiate intensive mothering. *Journal of Family Issues, 36*(3), 351–370.

Ellis-Sloan, K. (2014). Teenage mothers, stigma, and their 'presentations of self'. *Sociological Research Online, 19*(1), 1–13.

Fairclough, N. (1993). Critical discourse analysis and the marketization of public discourse: The universities. *Discourse & Society, 4*(2), 133–168.

Foucault, M. (1995). *Discipline and punish: The birth of the prison* (2nd ed., A. Sheridan, Trans.). Vintage Books. (Original work published 1977).

Foucault, M. (1978). *The history of sexuality*. Pantheon Books.

Foucault, M. (1991). Governmentality. In G. Burchell, C. Gordon, & P. Miller (Eds.), *The Foucault effect: Studies in governmentality* (pp. 87–104). University of Chicago Press.

Fraser, N., & Gordon, L. (1994). A genealogy of dependency: Tracing a keyword of the U.S. welfare state. *Signs: Journal of Women in Culture and Society, 19*(2), 309–336.

Geronimus, A. T. (2003). Damned if you do: Culture, identity, privilege, and teenage childbearing in the United States. *Social Science & Medicine, 57*(5), 881–893. doi:10.1016/S0277-9536(02)00456-2

Gregson, J. (2009). *The culture of teenage mothers*. SUNY Press.

Greyson, D., Chabot, C., & Shoveller, J. (2019). Young parents' experiences and perceptions of 'teen mom' reality shows. *Journal of Youth Studies, 22*(8), 1150–1165.

Greyson, D., O'Brien, H., & Shoveller, J. (2017). Constructing knowledge and ignorance in the social information worlds of young mothers. *Proceedings of the Association for Information Science and Technology, 54*(1), 139–149.

Harlan, M. A. (2016). Constructing youth: Reflecting on defining youth and impact on methods. *School Libraries Worldwide, 22*(2), 1–12.

Hays, S. (1996). *The cultural contradictions of motherhood*. Yale University Press.

Hermer, J., Kempa, M., Shearing, C., Stenning, P., & Wood, J. (2012). Policing in Canada in the twenty-first century: Directions for law reform. In D. Cooley (Ed.), *Re-imagining policing in Canada* (pp. 22–91). University of Toronto Press.

Kelly, D. M. (1998). Teacher discourses about a young parents program: The many meanings of "good choices". *Education and Urban Society, 30*(2), 224–241.

Kelly, D. M. (2000). *Pregnant with meaning: Teen mothers and the politics of inclusive schooling*. P. Lang.

Kirkman, M., Harrison, L., Hillier, L., & Pyett, P. (2001). 'I know I'm doing a good job': Canonical and autobiographical narratives of teenage mothers. *Culture, Health & Sexuality, 3*(3), 279–294.

Lesko, N. (1995). The 'leaky needs' of school-aged mothers: An examination of U.S. programs and policies. *Curriculum Inquiry, 25*(2), 177–205. doi:10.2307/1180186

Luttrell, W. (2003). *Pregnant bodies, fertile minds: Gender, race, and the schooling of pregnant teens*. Routledge.

McGregor, S. (2003). Critical discourse analysis: A primer. *Kappa Omicron Nu FORUM, 15*(1), 15–1. http://www.kon.org/archives/forum/15-1/mcgregorcda.html

McNay, L. (1992). *Foucault and feminism: Power, gender and the self*. Northeastern University Press.

Pillow, W. S. (2003). 'Bodies are dangerous': Using feminist genealogy as policy studies methodology. *Journal of Education Policy, 18*(2), 145–159.

Pillow, W. S. (2006). Teen pregnancy and education: Politics of knowledge, research, and practice. *Educational Policy, 20*(1), 59–84.

Pillow, W. S. (2015). Policy temporality and marked bodies: Feminist praxis amongst the ruins. *Critical Studies in Education, 56*(1), 55–70. doi:10.1080/17508487.2015.971331

Pomerantz, S. (2008). *Girls, style, and school identities: Dressing the part*. Palgrave.

Pomerantz, S., Raby, R., & Stefanik, A. (2013). Girls run the world? Caught between sexism and postfeminism in school. *Gender & Society, 27*(2), 185–207.

Prettyman, S. S. (2005). "We ain't no dogs": Teenage mothers (re)define themselves. In P. J. Bettis & N. G. Adams (Eds.), *Geographies of girlhood: Identities in-between* (pp. 155–173). Lawrence Erlbaum Associates.

Raby, R. (2012). Age: decentring adulthood. In D. Brock, R. Raby, & M. P. Thomas (Eds.), *Power and everyday practices* (pp. 133–156). Nelson.

Ringrose, J. (2006). A new universal mean girl: Examining the discursive construction and social regulation of a new feminine pathology. *Feminism & Psychology*, *16*(4), 405–424. doi:10.1177/0959353506068747

Salmon, A. (2007). Dis/abling states, dis/abling citizenship: Young Aboriginal mothers and the medicalization of fetal alcohol syndrome. *Journal for Critical Education Policy Studies*, *2*(5), 271–306.

SmithBattle, L. (2006). Helping teen mothers succeed. *The Journal of School Nursing*, *22*(3), 130–135. doi:10.1177/10598405060220030201

SmithBattle, L. (2007). 'I wanna have a good future': Teen mothers' rise in educational aspirations, competing demands, and limited school support. *Youth & Society*, *38*(3), 348–371.

SmithBattle, L., & Freed, P. (2016). Teen mothers' mental health. *MCN: The American Journal of Maternal/Child Nursing*, *41*(1), 31–36.

Spear, H. J. (2004). Personal narratives of adolescent mothers-to-be: Contraception, decision making, and future expectations. *Public Health Nursing*, *21*(4), 338–346. doi:10.1111/j.0737-1209.2004.21407.x

St. Pierre, E. (2000). Poststructural feminism in education: An overview. *International Journal of Qualitative Studies in Education*, *13*(5), 477–515.

Sukarieh, M., & Tannock, S. (2011). The positivity imperative: A critical look at the 'new' youth development movement. *Journal of Youth Studies*, *14*(6), 675–691. doi:10.1080/13676261.2011.571663

Tsaliki, L. (2015). Popular culture and moral panics about 'children at risk': Revisiting the sexualisation-of-young-girls debate. *Sex Education*, *15*(5), 500–514. doi:10.1080/14681811.2015.1022893

Tyyskä, V. (2014). Concepts and theories. In V. Tyyskä (Ed.), *Youth and society: The long and winding road* (3rd ed., pp. 1–22). Canadian Scholars' Press Inc.

Ussher, J. (2006). *Managing the monstrous feminine: Regulating the reproductive body*. Routledge.

van Dijk, T. A. (1995). Aims of critical discourse analysis. *Japanese Discourse*, *1*(1), 17–27.

Watson, L. L., & Vogel, L. R. (2017). Educational resiliency in teen mothers. *Cogent Education*, *4*(1), 1–22.

Weedon, C. (1987). *Feminist practice and poststructural theory*. Basil Blackwell.

Wigginton, B., & Lee, C. (2013). A story of stigma: Australian women's accounts of smoking during pregnancy. *Critical Public Health*, *23*(4), 466–481. doi:10.1080/09581596.2012.753408

Criminalization of Women Accessing Abortion and Enforced Mobility within the European Union and the United Kingdom

Lula Mecinska, Carolyne James, and Kate Mukungu

ABSTRACT

The article explores the impact of criminalization and restricted abortion access in Poland, Italy, and parts of the United Kingdom. We look at the ways in which the partial and extensive criminalization of abortion in the European Union and in the United Kingdom forces women to travel to access abortion care. At the core of our considerations is the interconnection of issues pertaining to criminalization and movement with citizenship, bodily integrity and autonomy, and the nation-state. By tracing these connections through an analysis of existing laws and scholarship, our concern here is to ask what discursive, narrative and theoretical resources feminist scholars might draw on and help co-produce in framing the interstices of criminalization of abortion and enforced mobility.

INTRODUCTION

Currently, no country in the EU effectively decriminalizes abortion, with varying degrees of acceptance for legal induced abortion grounds (Antoine, 2019; Berer, 2017; CECHR, 2018; COE, nd; Singh et al., 2018; World Health Organization, 2017). At present Malta is the only European Union state where abortion is fully outlawed with penalties between 18 months and three years of imprisonment (Center for Reproductive Rights, 2017; FRA, 2017; World Health Organization, 2018). Grounds for legal induced abortion remain severely limited in Poland, Cyprus, Finland, and in some countries and territories subject to UK laws (CRR, 2017; World Health Organization, 2018). However, even where restrictions may only be placed on the stage of pregnancy by which abortion is available, the complex legal and socio-political situation often creates a precarious situation for women seeking to access abortion care (Erdman, 2017; Fabbrini, 2011; Guillaume & Rossier, 2018). Indeed, in most countries, some form of penalties attached to abortion exists in the legal framework. Specific laws and their applications within EU member states and within their constituting nations variously produce a "chilling effect" on the possibility of obtaining a legal abortion (ECHR, 2019; Erdman, 2014, 2017). A further confounding element is a possibility, granted by law in 21 countries of the EU, for medical practitioners to invoke "conscientious objection" (CO) to performing an abortion (Heino et al., 2013). The existence of such a clause creates a further disadvantage for women based on their place of residence, socio-economic status, and income (Heino et al., 2013).

Partial and extensive criminalization of abortion in various parts of the EU forces pregnant people to travel to access abortion care to states or constituting nations in which induced abortion is legal and/or available. Termed variously "medical tourism" (Gilmartin & White, 2011), "abortion tourism" (Bloomer & O'Dowd, 2014; cf. Guillaume & Rossier, 2018) and, perhaps most accurately "reproductive exile" (Kasstan & Crook, 2018), this movement is *enforced* by the criminal justice systems of member states. Those unable to meet the demands of enforced travel attempt to procure abortions medically by illicitly buying "abortion pills" online (Berer, 2017; Guillaume & Rossier, 2018), often risking lengthy prison sentences. At the same time, the interplay between local and supranational (EU) laws has the potential to create tensions and—serendipitously for those affected—"inconsistencies within the domestic legal systems of those states which restrict abortion rights" (Fabbrini, 2011, p. 2). What we mean here, is how the rights to freedom of movement and freedom of access to services have been invoked and used as "leverage" in arguments against attempts to curtail travel for abortion care (Fabbrini, 2011; Human Rights Committee Secretariat, 2016). This contribution seeks to map out the consequences of partial and extensive criminalization of abortion in selected parts of the European Union and the United Kingdom, formerly an EU country and now in the process of separating itself ("Brexit"). The aim is to instigate a discussion on (un)intended consequences of criminal laws which write themselves on the bodies of women-citizens[1]. We are not looking at one specific group of women or different groups of women—rather, our approach at this stage in our collaborative endevor is to mark out the territory from an insider/outsider vantage point, within which we suggest a roadmap for future research directions. While the framework proposed provides a glance at the variegated landscapes where female bodies are criminalized, this contribution addresses current legal responses to women's reproductive rights in diverse settings. Putting forward a critical understanding of reproductive rights for women, we glance at the United Kingdom, Poland, and Italy to offer a panoramic view of how current abortion laws criminalize and undermine women's bodily autonomy. The concluding section returns to discourses that lead to abortion being posited as a threat to the life of society and challenges a strand in current theoretical writings on reproduction, which thus far tended to focus more on questions of subjectivity rather than the collective social identity that defines birth, reproductive rights, and citizenship for women.

CRIMINALIZING THE EMBODIED CITIZEN

The *de jure* and *de facto* criminalization of abortion across the EU and in the United Kingdom writes itself into a broader picture of heightened scrutiny, weaponized welfare oversight, and outright criminalization of women's bodies, and specifically pregnant bodies worldwide (Bloomer et al., 2019; Goodwin, 2017; OHCHR, 2017). While the principle of autonomy remains the basis of most conceptualizations of citizenship and has been deemed crucial for a feminist understanding of citizenship (Lister, 1997a, 1997b), under restrictive legislation on abortion, this autonomy is severely curtailed on the most basic, bodily level. Even though the law provides one of the primary tools for conceptualizing, promoting, and guarding women's autonomy, it also remains the chief arena in which the political tensions between demographic priorities and reproductive choices play out (cf. Freedman & Isaacs, 1993). Under the supranational regime of the European Union, a further tension exists between internationally derived standards and nationally enforced laws, often steeped in customs and religions of individual nation-states (Nowicka, 2011). Women's bodily autonomy and reproductive autonomy remain curtailed and with them, as many activists vocally argue (Antoine, 2019; Penny, 2019), women's full citizenship rights (cf. Horgan & O'Connor, 2014; Lakhani & Horgan, 2015). Furthermore, it is not simply that reproductive autonomy would enable women "to take control over their reproductive lives by entrusting to them both the authority to make decisions about reproduction and the ability to make those

[1]It is important to note that most laws regarding abortion remain specifically gendered; thus, while pregnancy and with it abortion care are issues of importance to transmasculine citizens, the specificity of the legal framework requires our attention to the category of 'women'.

decisions based on access to adequate information and suitable services" (Freedman & Isaacs, 1993, p. 19) but rather that "to force women to have children they do not wish to have is a form of violence against women" (Fried, 2016). We argue that the violence, enacted by the states, is also manifest in the expulsion that occurs when women have to travel in order to seek out abortion care, in what constitutes enforced migration. This migration, its criminalizing undercurrent, and the processes that cause it are not adequately captured through existing protocols, which tend to focus on discursively demarcated constructs of "migration" as a specific form of mobility (Gorodzeisky & Leykin, 2020).

OFFENSES AGAINST THE PERSON: THE MULTI-TERRITORIAL RIPPLES OF BRITISH-DERIVED LAWS

The complex picture of nation-state independent law-making on abortion is evident not only across, but often within individual states. Abortion in many of the territories currently dependent, associated with, or subsumed within the United Kingdom of Britain and Northern Ireland, and those formerly colonized by it[2], has been marked by section 58 and 59 of the Offenses Against the Person Act 1861, which provided penalties for women seeking the termination of a pregnancy and those who would assist them. The adoption of the 1967 Abortion Act in 1968 has made abortion more of an acceptable feature of life in *some* parts of the United Kingdom (Aiken et al., 2019; Greenwood, 2001). The Act applies to England, Wales, and Scotland and now Northern Ireland. The change of law has affected the Crown Dependencies—Jersey, Guernsey and Isle of Man—in as far as their residents were able to travel to the UK under the Common Travel Area to procure an abortion (Hansard, 1990), until it became lawful locally (1997, 1997, and 2019, respectively). In the British Overseas Territory of Gibraltar, the only such Territory surrounded by EU countries, abortion is regulated by section 11 of the Crime Act and punishable by life imprisonment—a not-too-distant echo of the "penal servitude for life" of section 58. Northern Ireland's situation remains, at the time of writing, unclear and in flux. A cross-party amendment passed in July 2019, compelling the government to decriminalize abortion in Northern Ireland and align the laws with the rest of the UK, became law in October 2019. Resulting provision is expected from April 2020 but is as yet undecided.

Importantly, the Abortion Act 1967 does not provide the right for the woman to end her pregnancy simply because she wants to, but rather gives registered medical practitioners (doctors) authority to decide whether there are medical grounds to support a woman's request for an abortion. section 1 of the Abortion Act made abortion legal when two doctors agreed in "good faith"—that is acting on the evidence presented to them or based on their own medical opinion—that pregnancy is less than twenty-four weeks[3] and evidence exists that the pregnancy would threaten the mother's life, her physical or mental health, or the unborn child would suffer "such physical or mental abnormalities as to be seriously handicapped," or that existing children would suffer harm. Significantly, the Abortion Act 1967 allows doctors to take into account the woman's "actual or reasonably foreseeable environment," that is her socio-economic conditions—a clause, which allows doctors to apply that element of the law with a significant amount of latitude. Arguably, if it had not been interpreted liberally by doctors who overwhelmingly proscribe to the view that it is damaging to the mental health of a woman to be forced to undergo a pregnancy against her will, the act would be unworkable in practice (Greenwood, 2001). This points to a

[2]In the formerly colonised Republic of Ireland, this law was further supplemented by the 8th Amendment of the Constitution of the Republic of Ireland giving equal rights to 'the unborn' as to the pregnant woman, with far-reaching consequences predicated on its legal and medical interpretations. The repeal of 'the 8th' in May 2018 can be seen as both a finishing point and an opening of a new chapter, in ROI's long march to reproductive freedom.

[3]In discrepancy with Infant Life (Preservation) Act 1929, which set the legal bounds for foetal viability and hence 'life' at 28 weeks.

risk, inherent in a law dependent on latitude in its application, and giving the ultimate decision, not to the woman, but an overseeing medical professional, as the same law could be used to restrict what is currently accessible (cf. Heino et al., 2013 and Italian case below).

The Act was, arguably, a product of its time, a result of concerns with reform and attempts to solve social problems through paternalistic welfare policies: a product of concerns over the effects of dangerous "back-street" abortions on the reproductive health of the nation and reverence to the medical authority which entrusted doctors as gatekeepers to a wide range of social and ethical decisions (BPAS, 2013; Greenwood, 2001; Sheldon, 2016). Such an attitude stands in stark contrast to current beliefs in which these choices belong to the patients (Sheldon, 2016). Purdy (2006) explains that a growing consensus respecting reproductive autonomy is the route to the ultimate advancement of women's welfare and Sheldon points out that women must be allowed to partake in the public domain on equivalent terms with men and that, "prima facie, control of one's own fertility is a fundamental prerequisite for such full participation" (Sheldon, 2016, p. 2).

Thus, it has to be of serious concern that the criminal law, the most formidable and authoritarian of state powers, can coercively control a woman's bodily autonomy and that invocation of such law can result in prosecution, punishment and even incarceration. It is important to understand that the 1967 Abortion Act does not legalize abortion but creates a range of exceptions to the 1861 Offenses Against the Person (OAP) Act. Potential criminal offenses apply to medical professionals who perform abortions and to women if they carry out an abortion on themselves (Brannan et al., 2017). Campaigners and practitioners argue that the restrictions in the law do not reflect the numerous changes in medical and clinical practice and they subvert the fundamental legal principles of bodily integrity (Article 3. HRA 1998) (Sheldon, 2016). A growing body of practitioners and campaigners within the UK, which include the British Medical Association, the Royal College of Obstetricians and Gynecologists (RCOG) and the Royal College of Midwifes (RCM) claim the law is archaic and out of date (Howard, 2017). Most specifically, the use of the drugs mifepristone and misoprostol up to the tenth week means abortions do not need to be monitored in a clinical setting (Guillaume & Rossier, 2018; Howard, 2017). In 2018 it was announced that women in England (following on from Scotland and Wales) will be allowed to take the second of the two drugs in their own homes. Scotland became the first part of the UK to allow women to take the "abortion pill" in their own homes, after the Chief Medical Officer (CMO), working in consultation with women-led organizations, had written to all Scottish health boards, with the backing of ministers, indicating that misoprostol could be taken outside a clinical setting (Chief Medical Officer Scotland, 2017). Although abortion law was devolved to Scotland under the post-independence referendum Scotland Act 2016, the CMO was using powers available under the existing Abortion Act 1967. Within the rationale for such an important milestone was the acknowledgment that women from rural and remote parts of Scotland were forced to travel long distances. This removal of just one journey, a small aspect of legally enforced mobility, was seen as a way to allow women to avoid the distress and embarrassment of bleeding and pain during a journey back from the hospital and vastly improve the experience of over 100,000 women a year (Cockerell, 2018).

Self-administered abortions using pills—often procured over the internet—was the cheapest, most accessible solution for women in Northern Ireland, who faced discrimination and inequality through the denial of equal access to abortion (Bloomer & O'Dowd, 2014). Until the recent changes in October 2019, abortion in Northern Ireland remained regulated by the 1861 OAP Act statute and the Criminal Justice Act 1945 (Northern Ireland), due to long-standing political resistance against any extension of the 1967 Act to Northern Ireland (Thomson, 2016). Rape, incest and severe fetal abnormality were not grounds for an abortion in Northern Ireland. As a result, women were forced either to accept unwanted pregnancies, risk criminal prosecution by purchasing abortion medication online, or travel to clinics in Britain to receive the healthcare they need—until June 2017 the NHS did not cover the costs of these abortions (Guillaume & Rossier, 2018; Hoctor et al., 2017). Further, in a glaring illustration of the Northern Irish paradox of enforcing mobility, within weeks of the Supreme Court ruling that the NHS did not have to provide them since the law of the land in Northern Ireland mostly forbade them, the charges associated with accessing abortion care were waived in England, Wales and Scotland, and the NHS concession approved by Parliament. Lawmakers were happy to put women on the move.

Activists in Northern Ireland have previously challenged the particular criminalization of women procuring abortion using pills by writing open communication to the Northern Ireland Police Service, stating they had used or supplied these pills. These acts of civil disobedience highlighted how unworkable the law is on this matter and challenged a change in the law by defying it (Lakhani & Horgan, 2015). Several well-publicized cases have brought the conflicted nature of NI legislation to the fore, among them a case of a 21-year-old woman, who in April 2016 was found guilty of having an abortion at 19 years old. The young woman was given a suspended prison sentence and her barrister stated that "had she lived in any other jurisdiction, in the UK, she would not have found herself before the court"—the young woman thus having been "victimized by the system" (McDonald, A., 2016; Mcdonald, H., 2016). Another is the case of a mother who in 2013 procured abortion pills online for her underage daughter (Lakhani & Horgan, 2015). After having accessed medical care for her deteriorating mental health, the young woman's medical records were shared with the Police. The 15-year-old was not prosecuted, but her mother faced two charges under the OAPA 1861 of unlawfully procuring poison (the abortion drugs) with intent to procure a miscarriage and supplying that poison to her daughter, facing a maximum sentence of 10 years. The day after the law changed on 23rd October 2019, she was formally acquitted at a Belfast Crown Court (Carroll, 2019) This underscores an inequality suffered by women in Northern Ireland: if the young woman had been living in any other part of the UK, she could have accessed these pills freely on the NHS (Amnesty International UK, 2019). This also reveals the hypocrisy of UK politics, which allows the prosecuting of women within the UK, whilst promoting universal access to sexual and reproductive health rights as a goal through its Department for International Development (Marie Stopes International, 2018).

Over the years, in the build-up to the change in the law in 2019, the UK has faced intense criticism and censure for failing to protect women in Northern Ireland. In February 2018, the UN Committee on the Elimination of Discrimination against Women (CEDAW) said that "the UK is responsible for "grave" and "systematic violations of women's rights in Northern Ireland" by constraining their access to abortion (OHCHR, 2018). In June 2018, the UK Supreme Court ruled that the law on abortion was incompatible with the right to respect for private and family life guaranteed by article 8 of the European Convention on Human Rights. Lord Mance stated the law is "untenable" and in need of "radical reconsideration" due to the "ongoing suffering" it causes (Supreme Court, 2018). In 2017 at least 861 women were forced to travel to England to access services that are legally available and readily accessible in all other parts of the UK (FPA, 2019). Lord Mance's description of the situation for women in Northern Ireland as "ongoing suffering" was not an understatement. There are multiple stories of the heartbreak and trauma caused to women and their families who faced unwanted or unviable pregnancies under the repressive regime (cf. Aiken et al., 2019; Horgan & O'Connor, 2014), which we can only hope is about to end. Despite the changes in the law, the actual nature of the provisions such as cut off dates, conscientious objection, and exclusion zones are yet to be established. However, the fact that women can now attend doctors' surgeries as patients and not as criminals is a radical, emancipatory and empowering change for women in Northern Ireland (Griffin, 2019).

LIMITING LEGAL ABORTION CARE, CRIMINALIZING SUPPORT, AND FETAL RIGHTS IN POLAND

Polish law on abortion in its current form has garnered public attention since 2016 due to repeated attempts to limit the existing restrictive provisions (Chrzczonowicz, 2017;

FEDERA, 2018a; Hoctor et al., 2017; Hugson, 2018; Korolczuk, 2016), which stem from the 1993 Act on Family Planning, Protection of the Human Fetus and Conditions of Acceptability of Abortion (JoL 1993, item 17 pos. 78). Currently, under the 1993 Act, legal access to induced abortion is limited to situations where the pregnancy poses a threat to the life or health of a pregnant woman, where prenatal tests or other medical indicators suggest a high probability of severe and irreversible impairment of the fetus or an incurable disease threatening its life, or when there is a reasonable suspicion that the pregnancy arose as a result of a prohibited act, such as incest, rape, and statutory rape. Unless the pregnancy poses an immediate threat to the woman's life, the first grounds have to be attested by a doctor other than the one who terminates the pregnancy. The same rule applies to the second grounds. In both, termination is available until the fetus is able to live independently outside the body of a pregnant woman. Most controversially, the third ground for legal abortion, available up to 12 weeks from conception, has to be attested by the public prosecutor's office.

The 1993 law the current basis of repression is often denoted a "compromise" between the religious fundamentalism of certain sections of the Roman Catholic Church in Poland and the country's progressive and left-leaning parties. But as Desperak (2003) observes, due to the discourse incited around the Act, reproductive rights and reproductive health have become politicized issues, and the Act itself can be read as an ideologized (and further ideologizing) instrument aimed at controlling women's bodies. The previously applicable law of 1956, which allowed for abortion due to "difficult living conditions" but left unspecified the determinants of such hardship and resulted in a liberal application of the law, was thus presented in political debate as a remnant of a "Soviet-inspired" mentality (Desperak, 2003; Korolczuk, 2016; Nowicka, 2011). There is no space here to discuss the full implications of the abortion laws as post/colonial legacies, which in itself is a detailed and extensive topic, but it is important to note this layer within the discursive practices around abortion laws and notions of "nationhood," where national identity—and with-it citizenship—may be forged as an alignment or difference with a significant other's attitudes (cf. Fletcher, 2001). The Polish political and legal landscape on abortion is therefore shaped by a combination of pro-natalist, religious and nationalist sentiments, resulting in a complex socio-legal discursive arena, where abortion is marked as a "foreign" concept.

Beyond limiting grounds for legal abortion, Poland also criminalizes terminations outside of these exceptions. The Act of June 6, 1997 - the Penal Code (Journal of Laws of 2017, item 2204, amended) Art 152 § 1 criminalizes providing a termination with a woman's consent and stipulates "deprivation of liberty for up to 3 years" as a sanction. The same penalty is provided by § 2 for offering or being persuaded to offer assistance to a woman in terminating a pregnancy outside the exceptions. The penalties for both reach up to 8 years for a fetus which "has reached the ability to live independently outside the body of a pregnant woman" (§ 3). Should a woman die as a result of an unlawfully procured abortion, the penalties range from 1 to 12 years imprisonment (Art. 154). Special provisions are made by Article 153 to the use of violence and coercion to influence a woman to terminate the pregnancy, and to terminations without a woman's consent. According to annual reports the number of prosecuted "abortion crimes" ranges between several dozen to several hundred per year; most cases involving the violation of art 152.2 of the Penal Code, concerning the provision of assistance to a woman in terminating a pregnancy, or persuading her to do so. Furthermore, in 1997, responding to an attempt to liberalize the 1993 Act, the Constitutional Tribunal ruled that The Constitution of the Republic of Poland in art. 38 posits "legal protection of human life," extending it to the category of "unborn child." As Janine P. Holc states, this decision problematically "situates 'unborn' citizens as privileged markers of the health of both democratic processes and the integrity of the nation" (Holc, 2004, p. 758). Discursively, this situates women advocating for abortion rights as "enemies" of the nation, state, and democracy, and aids to justify the expulsion of those seeking abortion care.

Polish law also stipulates a conscientious objection (CO) clause, under the art. 39 of the 1996 Act on the profession of doctor and dentist, which states that "a doctor may refrain from performing medical services inconsistent with their conscience (…) but is obliged to indicate an attainable way of obtaining the provision from another doctor or medical unit, and to justify and record this fact in the patient's medical documentation." In a joint letter from pro-choice organizations addressed to the Human Rights Committee Secretariat, the authors state that "the stark effects of the restrictive legal framework" which "combine to generate a punitive and stigmatizing environment" and have "a chilling effect for medical professionals," are further compounded by "a lack of effective regulation of conscience-based refusals of care" (Human Rights Committee Secretariat, 2016, pp. 2, 4). The authors of the letter also pointed to judgments of the European Court of Human Rights issued in three seminal cases against Poland which were a result of Poland's failure to guarantee in practice women's access to legal abortion services.[4] To further confound the picture, Desperak (2003, p. 197) notes that emergency contraception (EC) has also been branded as a tool for "early termination" within the national debates on abortion. Indeed, in one study, a high proportion of young women (68.3%) regarded EC as a means of early termination of pregnancy (Olszewski et al., 2007). Thus, despite its legality under EU provisions, the use of EC is reportedly increasingly blocked by CO doctors and pharmacists and monitored by law enforcement, a further layer of state-condoned disavowal of women's reproductive autonomy.

Between 2016 and 2018, proposals to ban and fully criminalize terminations, or to severely limit women's access to abortion were submitted to the Polish Parliament by citizen's initiatives (Sejm, 2017a, 2017b, 2018) and are in various ways proceeded in the Polish Parliament (FEDERA, 2018b). The 2016 "Stop Abortion" project seeks to instate a total ban on abortions and introduce criminal sanctions for the pregnant woman. Ostensibly rejected by parliament after "Black Protests" and pressure from the EU (Korolczuk, 2016; Nawojski, Pluta, & Zielinska, 2018), it has been sent to parliamentary committees using a legislative loophole.[5] Submitted soon after the 2017 "Halt Abortions" project by the Pro-Life Federation similarly seeks to ban abortions but without criminalizing women. It proposes to instate a ban on the right to abortion in the case of a high probability of a serious and irreversible impairment of the fetus or an incurable disease threatening its life. Its submission coincided with a challenge in the Constitutional Tribunal on the right to abortion in the case of irreversible impairments based on the "right to life" (Trybunal Konstytucyjny, 2017:K 13/17). While a pro-choice coalition "Save Women" submitted a counter project backed by 440,000 signatures, this was rejected by the Parliament in January 2018; the "Halt Abortion" project proceeded to parliamentary committees (FEDERA, 2018a). This demonstrates a consistent dedication on the part of lawmakers to maintaining the status quo, which forces women to seek abortion care outside legal bounds, either by traveling abroad or by avoiding the national healthcare system and going "underground" (Chełstowska, 2011).

Tracing the discursive changes that occurred alongside—and as an effect of—changes in the law and through the systematic campaigns by anti-choice organizations, Desperak (2003) notes the difficulty of framing abortion as a women's right. This, she agrees with Graff (2014), is due to the "disappearance of women" from the language used not only in official debate but also in popular media, including most women's magazines when discussing abortion. The radicalization of public discourse around abortion also means that women's organizations have for many years shied away from addressing the issue of legal abortion care, focusing instead on the availability of legally sanctioned "exceptions" (Desperak, 2003; Graff, 2014; Żuk & Żuk, 2017). Because of criminal sanctions placed on "assistance" even this form of intervention may be curtailed. In mid-2018, several women's organizations in Poland were informed of reports made to the authorities

[4]R.R. v. Poland, No. 27617/04 Eur. Ct. H.R., paras. 159-160 (2011); P. and S. v. Poland, No. 57375/0 Eur. Ct. H.R. (2012); Tysiaç v. Poland, No. 5410/03 Eur. Ct. H.R. (2007).

[5]In November 2016, Polish government approved a regulation offering pregnant women carrying a seriously disabled or unviable foetus a one-time payment of approx. €1,000 to carry the pregnancy to term.

by anti-choice organizations stipulating the possibility of crime being committed under article 152 of Penal Code, with information women's organizations publish about ways in which women can access legal abortions within and outside the country presented as "evidence" (FEDERA, 2018b).

It is important to note that there is currently no criminal sanction for the woman accessing abortion. This situation opens up the possibility to travel abroad to access abortion care. But the criminalization of assistance places women seeking to travel in a highly precarious situation. While official figures remain around 500–600 legal abortions a year, it is estimated that Polish women terminate around 150,000 pregnancies every year, and according to one CBOS study around 5.8 million Polish women have had an abortion (Swiechowicz, 2014, TVN24, 2014). Two separate simulation models for abortion rates in Poland suggest a realistic rate of between 30 and 185 thousand abortions annually (Ossowski, 2008). A proportion of these happens in the "abortion underground" in Poland—some through access to private providers, including medical professionals who are *not* trained obstetricians (Wojciechowski, 2016). Others through access and use of medication with known abortive properties, often purchased illegally online (Żuk & Żuk, 2017).

Increasingly both women and goods cross the boundaries of nation-states within the EU for the purposes of termination of pregnancy. Polish women typically travel to hospitals and clinics in countries where abortion is more freely available, primarily to nearby countries like Germany, Austria, Slovakia, and in rare cases in Lithuania, but they may also travel to the Netherlands, where abortion under "unbearable" circumstances is available until the 22 week, and less frequently to the UK (Gerdts et al., 2016). According to press reports, many clinics employ consultants who speak Polish (Swiechowicz, 2014) and some offer transport to and from the clinic; the lines of transit falling on routes that in the 1990s served trans-border traders and smugglers (cf. Gwiaździńska-Goraj & Jezierska-Thöle, 2013; Powęska, 2016). But with the costs of abortion with the transfer, the "problem" of abortion disproportionately affects poor women. As Krystyna Kacpura of the Federation for Women and Family Planning states "access to abortion depends on the depth of the wallets and resourcefulness of women" (Żuk & Żuk, 2017). Restricted mobility and state oversight affect women accessing abortion care and services, but increasingly also medication for medical abortions. Starting in January 2018 users of forums regarding legal access to contraception, emergency contraception (EC) and legal abortion began sharing experiences which point to an intensification of control over postal deliveries, reporting being questioned by the police (despite current laws permitting personal imports of up to five packets of EC pills) and being threatened with prosecution. In response, and as an act of open defiance, activist organizations re-staged pill-carrying drone flying exercises, crossing the river Oder from Germany into Polish territory. These examples point to the possibilities which supranational regulations open up (Fabbrini, 2011). Certainly, EU accession in 2004 and becoming part of the Schengen zone in 2007 have affected Polish women's access to abortion. The rights to freedom of movement and freedom of access to services have become welcome enabling factors, used as arguments *against* attempts to curtail travel for abortion care (Human Rights Committee Secretariat, 2016). The lack of border checks also remains an important factor enabling women to access abortion care in neighboring countries. However, in the current climate of increased border securitization and the proposed introduction of random medical testing, this freedom seems precarious. It nevertheless permits some liberal lawmakers to not address the issue by "outsourcing" it abroad.

LEGAL BUT INACCESSIBLE: ABORTION IN ITALY

The Italian abortion law (Law 22 May 1978, n. 194, *On the social protection of motherhood and the voluntary termination of pregnancy*, Gazzetta Ufficiale n. 140, 22 May 1978) reveals all the symptoms of ineffectiveness described in the previous cases. Popularly known as "Law 194," it leaves the decision regarding the permissibility of termination of pregnancy in the hands of the medical profession and allows doctors to opt-out of providing abortion on the grounds of conscience. In the forty years of its existence, the application of the law by doctors whose consciences continue to be affected by the Roman Catholic Church and its considerable political power has made it less available than the law on paper would suppose (Hanafin, 2007; Caruso, 2020) forcing women to move in search of non-objecting practitioners. As is the case in Poland, the prevailing law is the result of a "compromise" between the two dominant parties at the time of its introduction—the Christian Democrats and the Communist Party—signaled in the first article of the law by the reference to the protection of "human life from inception" and "social value of maternity," whilst also highlighting the state's role in guaranteeing "responsible procreation." This discursive pattern reveals a tension within the law itself between (female) citizen's bodily autonomy and Italy's patriarchal values (Hanafin, 2007). It is further exacerbated by Article 37 of the Italian constitution, which reiterates the primacy of the maternal role for women (Andall, 1994). Despite attempts by the feminist movement in Italy to secure a more woman-centric and self-sufficient model for abortion care at its inception (Caruso, 2020; Hanafin, 2007), current provisions under Law 194 and right to CO are severely restricted in practice. As a result, women are forced to travel to access abortion care—this enforced movement occurs both within the country's regions or between them, and abroad (Gerdts et al., 2016).

While Law 194 permits "interruption" of pregnancy during the first 90 days on a "voluntary" (or better "volitional" basis, Article 4), this must be predicated on health, economic, family or personal reasons (Caruso, 2020; Chavkin et al., 2017). Under Article 6, terminations up to 24 weeks gestation are only permissible in cases of serious danger to a woman's life or when fetal abnormalities pose a risk to her physical and mental health (Caruso, 2020; Chavkin et al., 2017). The pregnancy, and the woman's physical and mental health, need to be assessed by a physician. Importantly the woman may choose the provider and the facility, but the decision is in the physician's hands. Women under 18 years of age may additionally require the permission of their legal guardian or parent, or a judicial decree (Article 12). The doctor may declare the need for abortion "urgent," which grants the woman access to termination without delay. More typically they will be bound by Article 5 to note the woman's stated reasons for termination, issuing a document, which attests that the woman is pregnant and "invites her to reflect for seven days" (Caruso, 2020) creating the first push to move around and find a supportive practitioner. This document is a certificate confirming the woman's qualification for the procedure, which is free for women who have the state healthcare system *tessera sanatoria* insurance card; women without the card are required to cover the cost of the procedure (Edwards, 2018). While the services are publicly funded, the law limits the provision to accredited centers and/or public hospitals and introduces administrative sanctions (fines) for women who seek self-funded abortions from private providers (Articles 8, 9). The latter also covers self-management of abortion with the use of abortifacients and pills. The introduction of procedural steps effectively curtails many women's ability to access abortion care within the legal limits. As a result, women seeking an abortion after 12 weeks might be forced to travel abroad for care—including the UK (Gerdts et al., 2016). Those who do not have the means, increasingly resort to illegal, potentially risky abortions. A legislative decree de-penalizing secret and illegal abortion was introduced in 2016 in response to activist interventions. At the same time, however, the Cabinet of Ministers increased the financial penalty for those to up to €10,000.

Several of the law's provisions for legally permissible abortion make the law unworkable and reflect what Andall (1994, p. 244) terms an "ideological attachment to a specific vision of women's appropriate role." In the legal arena, patriarchal familialism was one of the pillars of Italian fascism (Andall, 1994; Caruso, 2020; Hanafin, 2007). Several authors note that the symbolic legal construction of women as reproducers of the nation reflects how little has changed in the relationship between the state and its women-citizens in Italy's postwar period. Right-leaning groups have consistently attempted to challenge Law 194, for the first time in 1981 when the Right to Life Movement was formed and collected enough signatures to propose a referendum repealing the abortion act (Andall, 1994; Hanafin, 2007). Of those voting, 68% were against the motion.[6] Despite this clear confirmation of popular support, successive challenges ensued, most notably on the back of legislation on bioethics with the Christian Democratic government proposing the introduction of Catholic counselors to abortion clinics (Andall, 1994). Their role was to specifically counsel women against abortions, over and beyond the currently required "options counselling." The stated purpose of the counsel (Article 5) is to make women aware of available welfare strategies, with the father of the *concepito* (the conceived) involved at the woman's permission. This fits with the broader opposition toward women's self-determination and the familialism of Italian law, where the good of the family is valued over and above that of its individual members (Andall, 1994). An understandable wish to avoid these confrontations would again require travel.

Another push to travel in search of abortion care occurs internally, between the country's regions, and applies equally to women seeking terminations and to doctors willing to provide it. Article 9 of Law 194 provides a clause allowing medical personnel conscientious objection through a declaration made to the provincial medical officer, which can be submitted and canceled at any time (Caruso, 2020). As a result, gynecologists, but also nurses, anesthetists and other assistants, can refuse to provide legally sanctioned abortion care, unless the immediate termination is needed in order to save the woman's life (Chavkin et al., 2017; Ministero della Salute, 2018; Torrisi, 2017). The annual reports by the Italian Ministry of Health (Ministero della Salute) on Law 194 indicate CO has been declared by just over 70% of the country's gynecologists, with as many as 93% in Molise, and around 80% in Sicily and Rome and the surrounding Lazio region. Nevertheless, the Ministry is at pains to stress that for the women 92.1% of terminations took place "in the region of residence" (Ministero della Salute, 2018). This does not account for travel times for rural women, a measure postulated by researchers in the medical field as a better qualifier of access barriers than distance (Barr-Walker et al., 2019). The seemingly low mobility of women also hides the reported pressures on the medical professionals, who not only experience discrimination, increased workloads, and limited career trajectories but may also face relocation—leading some to record CO to avoid uprooting (Chavkin et al., 2017, De Zordo 2018). Finally, with many public hospitals affiliated with the RCC, even non-objectors may find it impossible to provide adequate care (Pianigiani, 2016; Tamma, 2018). Italy's case of enforced mobility is thus brought about through its laws on CO.

It has been argued that the law exhibits all the problems inherent in attempting to transform women's legal position without a transformation in the symbolic position of women (Hanafin, 2007). Just as forty years ago, the efforts of the women's movement still concentrate on women's self-determination and ability to access to safe abortion care. With medical abortion an outpatient procedure in only 5 of the country's 20 regions and still managed by hospitals (Edwards, 2018), chances of any swift changes are low. Enforced travel for women results in shame and stigmatization, posing also a risk to health and presenting a financial burden. Marginalized women—those living in poverty, uninsured, migrants and asylum-seekers—or those simply too ill to travel are often forced to turn to clandestine and potentially dangerous methods. Social Rights Committee of the Council of Europe agreed with the complaint brought forward by Italy's biggest union CGIL (Italian General Confederation of Labor) in 2016, stating that as a result of widespread conscientious objection limiting access to safe abortion services women's rights were being violated by Italy (Reuters, 2016). Hanafin (2007, p. 1) cites Haraway (1990), arguing that the

[6]Simultaneously, the Radical Party was able to put forward a referendum expanding the law to private providers and improving provision for minors; this was defeated with 88% voting against the motion (Andall 1994).

Italian case illustrates how "reproductive politics is at the heart of questions about citizenship, liberty, family, and nation." Questions around citizenship emerge through the valorization of rights of fetuses over those of women, liberty is put in question by the denial of self-determination, the family is proscribed through the law's explicit references to the heteropatriarchal model, and national values are equated with those of the RCC, as reflected in the constitution. At the level of provision of abortion care, this is demonstrated by the balancing act of CO within a public healthcare system. As argued by Chavkin, Swerdlow and Fifield (2017) "legally permissible CO to legally sanctioned health care" reveals the tensions within societies committed to delivering democratically agreed national healthcare services between the interests of women-citizens seeking abortion care, the willing providers, the objectors and the political powers that bind them. The current law has been ineffective in changing the symbolic position of women and obscures their exploitation as intended reproducers of the nation (Caruso, 2020; Irigaray, 1985) or forces them to travel to assert their self-determination.

MAPPING CONNECTIONS AND ENGAGING IN ACTIVISM

Across the contexts described here, different laws curtailing access to or criminalizing abortion directly or indirectly, remain in place as women are forced to seek "ways around" them in order to access abortion care. Human rights bodies have repeatedly held that restrictive abortion laws violate women's and girls' rights to life, health, privacy, nondiscrimination and freedom from torture and other ill-treatment (Chavkin et al., 2017). Similarly, withholding and denial of abortion-related information to women also violate our fundamental human rights. Yet it seems some states care little for the autonomy of their women-citizens, and little perhaps for their health, as they are satisfied to effectively "outsource" abortion care to contexts outside their jurisdiction, by privatizing and exterritorializing its reality. By addressing contexts and meanings pertaining to the criminalization of abortion we challenge the way in which reproduction is theorized - the reproductive discourse about women "without women" (Arendt, 1958). Laws regulating abortion outline intimate aspects of "private" life as matters of intense public regulatory interest and represent, preferably marital, (hetero)sex as an activity involving the production of citizens (Caruso, 2020; Nawojski et al., 2018). The underlying legal argument remains that regulation of private conduct becomes necessary to preserve the character of public life (Nawojski et al., 2018). This is to say that abortion does not simply threaten the unborn; it threatens unborn populations (cf. Siegel, 1992). Arguments against abortion represent family and state in traditional, homologous relation to each other, where they are both interdependent institutions (Caruso, 2020; Desperak, 2003; Graff, 2014). Furthermore, the widespread claim that life begins at conception provides a persuasive basis for criminalizing abortion, as one of many arguments that identify the reproductive process as the basis of social life (Desperak, 2003). Such rhetoric has been employed against abortion for a long time (Siegel, 1992) and used to put forward the argument that regulating the physical act of reproduction is necessary to guarantee and safeguard the reproduction of the social order. Consequently, as we see in the cases described, subjects who are involved in the act of abortion are subjected to enforced mobility. Rather than an individual issue, abortion becomes a "blemish" on the body politic (Siegel, 1992).

This exclusion/expulsion materializes in the criminalization of abortion and the enforced mobility it produces. The mobility necessary to access abortion care becomes a double (triple?) transgression: of laws criminalizing abortion and of boundaries of national belonging and allegiance to a reproductive future. By the same token, through enforced mobility, the states involved in the expulsion of their citizens 'absolve themselves' from the responsibility for the act of abortion.

Although recourse to international instruments and human rights laws has proven successful in some cases (Bloomer et al., 2019), it is also important to note that sometimes supranational affordances—such as the EU freedom of movement—may also present hindrances to localized change. While "freedom of movement" allows women to retain shreds of dignity and autonomy, it allows states to outsource reproductive services. One potential response is the insistence of intra-state and cross-border parity, as was the case for the "Now for NI" campaign (BPAS, 2015). Coordinated transnational actions and activism, establishing connections with grassroots movements, facilitated by digital organizing have allowed for acts of solidarity that allow each campaign to reach further than it ever has, as exemplified by the resonance of the Polish Black Protest initiated in September 2016. Cullen and Korolczuk (2019) and Bloomer et al. (2019, p. 89) argue that transnational, digitally enabled, feminist activism allows us to "witness the global nature of control of women's reproductive lives and often the similar forms it takes [and] provides a global solidarity movement" whilst remaining situated in local contexts.

As activists seek to engage in various forms of action, we uphold that as scholars, we need to embrace and support activism. Feminists and other critical theorists have long held that the construction of knowledge is a political process and Italian feminist thinkers have woven a useful reworking of theory/praxis relationship (Hanafin, 2007), proposing an un-thinking/un-doing of the dominant power structures and traditional politics (Caruso, 2020). As demonstrated most recently, in the cases of Ireland and Poland, academic considerations of abortion could support activist groups by using the political process of knowledge-making to gather evidence to inform and enrich activism (cf de Londras & Enright, 2018; Korolczuk, 2016) and evidence ways that travel to access abortion care creates risks to women's health, generates costs and presents logistical problems (Bloomer et al., 2019). Beyond that, the haunting prospect of a movement that never ends, and of a pain that cannot find an outlet can, and has been, used as a powerful tool to dismantle the laws or to oppose restrictions. Highlighting the pain of being banished abroad to deal with a crisis pregnancy, became a key feature of the campaign to repeal the 8th Amendment in the Republic of Ireland and abortion reform in Northern Ireland, and remains the focus of current Polish campaigning. Those stories—mobilized in challenging restrictive laws—also travel; shared between national contexts, they turn private tragedies into accounts of state-enforced violence and injustice. In The Republic of Ireland and Northern Ireland, campaign efforts involved many people going public with their abortion stories, including those from the group TMFR (Termination for Medical Reasons) and those sharing their stories anonymously as part of the multi-platform "In Her Shoes" campaign. In Poland, the story of using pills and then seeking abortion abroad recounted by the singer Natalia Przybysz galvanized public opinion. Beyond humanizing peoples' experiences and revealing the injustice of the law, telling stories of the unsafe situations and risks pregnant women endure when procuring an abortion abroad or using pills and being afraid to seek medical help in discomfort or distress, helped to highlight the headline that criminalization was bad for women's health, dangerous to women's lives and amounts to state-sanctioned violence against women. But such testimonies also highlighted how those within borders as asylum seekers had to endure enforced immobility when faced with crisis pregnancies, an issue warranting a separate paper. The activism allowed for the emergence of arguments around access to EC and to medical abortion under WHO "Model List of Essential Medication" (cf Bloomer et al., 2019). Most significantly, effective campaigning built its strength not on allegiance to a nation-state, but on disrupting this allegiance, by standing on the side of those breaking the law. Polish activists have, for example, defiantly flown drones with pills from Germany, mobilizing resistance and visualizing the movement and posed on the cover of a women's glossy in T-shirts stating, "Abortion is OK."

Women do and will risk everything when faced with an unwanted pregnancy—criminalization is neither effective nor is it just. One of the main contributions of women's organizing focused on re-telling of stories and challenging of enforced mobility has been the dismantling of abortion stigma, which marked women accessing abortion care as failing to attain "the ideal of 'womanhood'" (Kumar, 2009 in Bloomer et al., 2019, p. 56). In all the contexts discussed, campaigners reminded the public that it was highly likely they knew a woman who had an abortion and that she was likely to be their mother, sister, or friend. Such public attempts to resist the stigma aim to wrestle the discourse around abortion back into women's control. We include our voices in that anti-stigma momentum, as well as our critique of states who wish to distort and criminalize the reality of abortion. This is the path we must stay on.

ORCID

Lula Mecinska http://orcid.org/0000-0002-0741-130X
Kate Mukungu http://orcid.org/0000-0003-3403-8165

REFERENCES

Aiken, A., Padron, E., Broussard, K., & Johnson, D. (2019). The impact of Northern Ireland's abortion laws on women's abortion decision-making and experiences. *BMJ Sexual & Reproductive Health*, *45*(1), 3–9. https://doi.org/10.1136/bmjsrh-2018-200198

Amnesty International UK. (2019). *Northern Ireland: Concern as mother who bought abortion pills for daughter to face criminal trial*. Amnesty. https://www.amnesty.org.uk/press-releases/northern-ireland-concern-mother-who-bought-abortion-pills-daughter-face-criminal

Andall, J. (1994). Abortion, politics and gender in Italy. *Parliamentary Affairs*, *47*(2), 238–252. https://doi.org/10.1093/oxfordjournals.pa.a052468

Antoine, P. (2019, July 24). Europe's patchwork of abortion laws is absurd. Rights must be made universal. The Guardian Online. https://www.theguardian.com/commentisfree/2019/jul/24/europe-abortion-laws-germany

Arendt, H. (1958). *The human condition*. Routledge.

Barr-Walker, J., Jayaweera, R. T., Ramirez, A. M., & Gerdts, C. (2019). Experiences of women who travel for abortion: A mixed methods systematic review. *PLoS One*, *14*(4), e0209991. https://doi.org/10.1371/journal.pone.0209991

Berer, M. (2017). Abortion law and policy around the world: In search of decriminalization. *Health and Human Rights*, *19*(1), 13–27.

Bloomer, F., & O'Dowd, K. (2014). Restricted access to abortion in the Republic of Ireland and Northern Ireland: Exploring abortion tourism and barriers to legal reform. *Culture, Health & Sexuality*, *16*(4), 366–380. https://doi.org/10.1080/13691058.2014.886724

Bloomer, F., Pierson, C., & Claudio, S. E. (2019). *Reimagining global abortion politics: A social justice perspective*. Policy Press.

BPAS. (2013). *Britain's Abortion Law What it says, and why*. British Pregnancy Advisory Service. http://www.reproductivereview.org/images/uploads/Britains_abortion_law.pdf

BPAS. (2015). *Britain's abortion law*. British Pregnancy Advisory Service. https://www.bpas.org/get-involved/campaigns/briefings/abortion-law/

Brannan, S., Campbell, R., English, V., Mussell, R., Sheather, J. C., & Davies, M. (2017). Ethics briefing. *Journal of Medical Ethics*, *43*(10), 723–724. https://doi.org/10.1136/medethics-2017-1044

Carroll, R. (2019, October 23). Woman in Northern Ireland abortion pills case formally acquitted. The Guardian, https://www.theguardian.com/uk-news/2019/oct/23/woman-northern-ireland-abortion-pills-case-formally-acquitted-legal-reforms

Caruso, E. (2020). Abortion in Italy: Forty years on. *Feminist Legal Studies*, https://doi.org/10.1007/s10691-019-09419-w

Center For Reproductive Rights. (2017). *The world's abortion laws*. CFRR. http://worldabortionlaws.com/

Center for Reproductive Rights. (2018). *Malta*. CFRR. https://reproductiverights.org/country/malta

Chavkin, W., Swerdlow, L., & Fifield, J. (2017). Regulation of conscientious objection to abortion: An international comparative multiple-case study. *Health and Human Rights*, *19*(1), 55.

Chełstowska, A. (2011). Stigmatisation and commercialisation of abortion services in Poland: turning sin into gold. *Reproductive Health Matters*, *19*(37), 98–106. https://doi.org/10.1016/S0968-8080(11)37548-9

Chief Medical Officer Scotland. (2017). *Abortion - Improvement to existing services – Approval for misoprostol to be taken at home*. Chief Medical Officer Directorate. https://www.sehd.scot.nhs.uk/cmo/CMO(2017)14.pdf

Chrzczonowicz, M. (2017, June 18). Całkowity zakaz aborcj i iwięzienie za antykoncepcję awaryjną – projekt wraca do Sejmu. Co zrobi PiS? OKO Press. https://oko.press/calkowity-zakaz-aborcji-wiezienie-antykoncepcje-awaryjna-projekt-wraca-sejmu-zrobi-pis/

Cockerell, M. (2018, August 25). Women in England to be allowed to take second early abortion pill at home. The Independent. https://www.independent.co.uk/news/health/misoprostol-at-home-england-women-early-abortion-new-law-a8506971.html

Council of Europe Commissioner for Human Rights. (2018). *Muižnieks: Need to reform abortion law in Malta*. Council of Europe Commissioner for Human Rights. https://www.coe.int/fr/web/commissioner/test/-/asset_publisher/Rm1SRoqfe8BH/content/need-to-reform-abortion-law?inheritRedirect=false

Council of Europe Commission on Human Rights. (n.d.). *Women's sexual and reproductive health and rights in Europe*. CECHR. https://www.coe.int/en/web/commissioner/women-s-sexual-and-reproductive-rights-in-europe

Cullen, P., & Korolczuk, E. (2019). Challenging abortion stigma: Framing abortion in Ireland and Poland. *Sexual and Reproductive Health Matters*, *27*(3), 6–19. https://doi.org/10.1080/26410397.2019.1686197

De Londras, F., & Enright, M. (2018). *Repealing the 8th Reforming Irish Abortion Law*. Policy Press.

De Zordo, S. (2018). From women's 'irresponsibility' to foetal 'patienthood': Obstetricians-gynaecologists' perspectives on abortion and its stigmatisation in Italy and Cataluña. *Global Public Health*, *13*(6), 711–723. https://doi.org/10.1080/17441692.2017.1293707

Desperak, I. (2003). Antykoncepcja, aborcja i… eutanazja. O upolitycznieniu prawreprodukcyjnych w Polsce [Contraception, Abortion and…. Euthanasia. On politicisation of reproductive rights in Poland]. *Folia Sociologica*, *30*, 194–207.

Edwards, C. (2018, May 25). The long road to legal abortion in Italy - and why many women are still denied it. The Local. https://www.thelocal.it/20180525/history-abortion-laws-italy-doctors-objection-pills

Erdman, J. N. (2014). Procedural abortion rights: Ireland and the European Court of Human Rights. *Reproductive Health Matters*, *22*(44), 22–30. https://doi.org/10.1016/S0968-8080(14)44798-0

Erdman, J. N. (2017). Theorizing time in abortion law and human rights. *Health and Human Rights*, *19*(1), 29–40. https://www.ncbi.nlm.nih.gov/pmc/articles/PMC5473036/

European Commission on Human Rights [ECHR]. (2019). *Reproductive rights Factsheet: Access to abortion*. ECHR. https://www.echr.coe.int/Documents/FS_Reproductive_ENG.pdf

Fabbrini, F. (2011). The European Court of Human Rights, the EU Charter of Fundamental Rights and the right to abortion: Roe v. Wade on the Other Side of the Atlantic? *Columbia Journal of European Law*, *18*(1), 1–72.

FEDERA. (2018a). *Stanowisko ws. pomocnictwa przyaborcji*. Federation for Women and Family Planning. http://federa.org.pl/pomocnictwo/

FEDERA. (2018b). *Barbarian anti-abortion bill back in the fundamentalists' game*. Federation for Women and Family Planning. http://en.federa.org.pl/barbarian-anti-abortion-bill-back-in-the-game/

Fletcher, R. (2001). Post-colonial fragments: Representations of abortion in Irish law and politics. *Journal of Law and Society*, *28*(4), 568–579. https://doi.org/10.1111/1467-6478.00203

FRA. (2017). *Accessing abortion services*. FRA. https://fra.europa.eu/en/publication/2017/mapping-minimum-age-requirements/access-abortion-services

FPA. (2019). *Why Abortion Law reform is needed*. FPA. https://www.fpa.org.uk/sexual-and-reproductive-rights/abortion-rights/abortion-in-northern-ireland/why-change-in-law-needed

Freedman, L., & Isaacs, S. (1993). Human rights and reproductive choice. *Studies in Family Planning*, *24*(1), 18–30. https://doi.org/10.2307/2939211

Fried, S. (2016, September 30). *Women's bodily integrity: linking criminalisation of abortion and criminalisation of HIV*. Human rights reproductive, maternal, neonatal and child health. https://marlin-prod.literatumonline.com/pb-assets/Lancet/langlo/TLGH_Blogs_2013-2018.pdf

Gerdts, C., DeZordo, S., Mishtal, J., Barr-Walker, J., & Lohr, P. A. (2016). Experiences of women who travel to England for abortions: An exploratory pilot study. *The European Journal of Contraception & Reproductive Health Care*, *21*(5), 401–407. https://doi.org/10.1080/13625187.2016.1217325

Gilmartin, M., & White, A. (2011). Interrogating medical tourism: Ireland, abortion, and mobility rights. *Signs: Journal of Women in Culture and Society*, *36*(2), 275–280. https://doi.org/10.1086/655907

Goodwin, M. (2017). How the criminalization of pregnancy robs women of reproductive autonomy. *Hastings Center Report*, *47*(6), S19–S27. https://doi.org/10.1002/hast.791

Gorodzeisky, A., & Leykin, I. (2020). When borders migrate: Reconstructing the category of 'international migrant'. *Sociology*, *54*(1), 142–158. https://doi.org/10.1177/0038038519860403

Graff, A. (2014). Report from the gender trenches: War against 'genderism' in Poland. *European Journal of Women's Studies*, *21*(4), 431–435. https://doi.org/10.1177/1350506814546091

Greenwood, J. (2001). The new ethics of abortion. *Journal of Medical Ethics*, *27*(2), ii2–ii4. https://doi.org/10.1136/jme.27.suppl_2.ii2

Griffin, N. (2019). Patients, not criminals: Northern Ireland grapples with how to provide legal abortion. *BMJ*, *367*, l6318. https://www.bmj.com/content/367/bmj.l6318.full

Guillaume, A., & Rossier, C. (2018). L'avortement dans le monde. État des lieux des législations, mesures, tendances et consequences [Abortion Around the World. An Overview of Legislation, Measures, Trends, and Consequences]. *Population*, *73*(2), 225–306. https://www.cairn.info/revue-population-2018-2-page-225.htm.

Gwiaździńska-Goraj, M., & Jezierska-Thöle, A. (2013). Modele rozwoju sektora usługowego małych miast w polskiej strefie przygranicznej z Niemcami i Rosją (ObwódKaliningradzki). [Models of the development of the service sector of small towns in the Polish border zone with Germany and Russia (Kaliningrad)]. *Folia Geographica Socio-Oeconomica*, *15*, 39–60.

Hanafin, P. (2007). *Conceiving life: Reproductive politics and the law in contemporary Italy*. Ashgate.

Hansard. (1990). *Abortion*. UK Parliament. https://api.parliament.uk/historic-hansard/written-answers/1990/jul/26/abortion

Haraway, D. (1990). *Modest_Witness@Second_Millennium*. FemaleMan_Meets_OncoMouse: Feminism and Technoscience. Routledge.

Heino, A., Gissler, M., Apter, D., & Fiala, C. (2013). Conscientious objection and induced abortion in Europe. *The European Journal of Contraception & Reproductive Health Care*, *18*(4), 231–233. https://doi.org/10.3109/13625187.2013.819848

Hoctor, L., Lamačková, A., & Thomasen, K. (2017). *Women's sexual and reproductive health and rights in Europe*. Council of Europe. https://rm.coe.int/women-s-sexual-and-reproductive-health-and-rights-in-europe-issue-pape/168076dead

Holc, J. P. (2004). The purest democrat: Foetal citizenship and subjectivity in the construction of democracy in Poland. *Signs: Journal of Women in Culture and Society*, *29*(3), 755–782. https://doi.org/10.1086/381106

Horgan, G., & O'Connor, J. S. (2014). Abortion and Citizenship Rights in a Devolved Region of the UK. *Social Policy and Society*, *13*(1), 39–49. https://doi.org/10.1017/S1474746413000146

Howard, S. (2017). After 50 years of legal abortion in Great Britain, calls grow for further liberalisation. *British Medical Journal, Obstetrics and Gynaecology*, *359*, j5278.

Hugson, G. (2018, August 31). The struggle for sexual and reproductive health and rights in central and eastern Europe. *NAM*. https://www.aidsmap.com/news/aug-2018/struggle-sexual-and-reproductive-health-and-rights-central-and-eastern-europe

Human Rights Committee Secretariat. (2016, September 22). *Supplemental information on Poland for the periodic review by the human rights committee at its 118th session (17 October 2016 - 4 November 2016)*. HRCS. https://tbinternet.ohchr.org/Treaties/CCPR/Shared%20Documents/POL/INT_CCPR_CSS_POL_25283_E.docx

Irigaray, L. (1985). *This sex which is not one*. Routledge.

Kasstan, B., & Crook, S. (2018). Reproductive rebellions in Britain and the Republic of Ireland: Contemporary and past abortion activism and alternative sites of care. *Feminist Encounters: A Journal of Critical Studies in Culture and Politics*, *2*(2), 2542–4920. https://doi.org/10.20897/femenc/3885

Korolczuk, E. (2016). Explaining mass protests against abortion ban in Poland: The power of connective action. *Zoon Politikon*, 7, 91–113.

Lakhani, N., & Horgan, G. (2015). Pregnant, in danger and scared to speak: Abortion laws and social stigma in El Salvador and Ireland. *Index on Censorship*, *44*(4), 29–33. https://doi.org/10.1177/0306422015622929

Lister, R. (1997a). *Citizenship: Feminist perspectives*. NYU Press.

Lister, R. (1997b). Citizenship: Towards a feminist synthesis. *Feminist Review*, *57*(1), 28–48. https://doi.org/10.1080/014177897339641

Marie Stopes International. (2018). *New flagship health programme to transform the lives of millions of women and girls*. MSI. https://mariestopes.org/news/2018/11/new-flagship-health-programme-to-transform-the-lives-of-millions-of-women-and-girls-and-accelerate-fp2020-progress

McDonald, A. (2016, April 22). Northern Ireland woman who bought abortion pills given suspended prison sentence. Belfast Telegraph. https://www.belfasttelegraph.co.uk/news/northern-ireland/northern-ireland-woman-who-bought-abortion-pills-given-suspended-prison-sentence-34597487.html

McDonald, H. (2016, April 4). Northern Irish woman given suspended sentence over self-induced abortion. The Guardian. https://www.theguardian.com/uk-news/2016/apr/04/northern-irish-woman-suspended-sentence-self-induced-abortion

Ministero della Salute. (2018). *Relazione del Ministro della Salute sulla attuazione della legge contenente norme per la tutela sociale della maternità e per l'interruzione volontaria di gravidanza (Legge 194/78)*. Ministry of Health.

Nawojski, R., Pluta, M., Zielinska, K. (2018). The black protests: A struggle for (re)definition of intimate citizenship. *Praktyka Teoretyczna*, *4*(30), 51–74. https://doi.org/10.14746/prt.2018.4.2

Nowicka, W. (2011). Sexual and reproductive rights and the human rights agenda: Controversial and contested. *Reproductive Health Matters*, *19*(38), 119–128. https://doi.org/10.1016/S0968-8080(11)38574-6

OHCHR. (2017). *Women's autonomy, equality and reproductive health in international human rights: Between recognition, backlash and regressive trends. Working Group on the issue of discrimination against women in law and in practice*. UN. https://www.ohchr.org/Documents/Issues/Women/WG/WomensAutonomyEqualityReproductiveHealth.pdf

OHCHR. (2018). *UK violates women's rights in Northern Ireland by unduly restricting access to abortion – UN experts*. UN. https://www.ohchr.org/en/NewsEvents/Pages/DisplayNews.aspx?NewsID=22693&LangID=E

Olszewski, J., Olszewska, H., Abacjew, A., Chmylko, L., & Gaworska-Krzeminska, A. (2007). The use of emergency contraception in young Polish women. *Acta Obstetricia et Gynecologica Scandinavica*, *86*(7), 861–869. https://doi.org/10.1080/00016340701416960

Ossowski, L. (2008). An attempt to simulate the number of abortions in Poland using data of selected European countries. *Studia Demograficzne*, *1*, 112–137.

Penny, L. (2019, May 18). The criminalization of women's bodies is all about conservative male power. The New Republic. https://newrepublic.com/article/153942/criminalization-womens-bodies-conservative-male-power

Pianigiani, G. (2016, January 16). On paper, Italy allows abortions, but few doctors will perform them. The New York Times. https://www.nytimes.com/2016/01/17/world/europe/on-paper-italy-allows-abortions-but-few-doctors-will-perform-them.html.

Powęska, H. (2016). *Handel przygraniczny w warunkach zmian przenikalności granicy [Border trade in the conditions of changes in permeability of the border]*. Wydawnictwo SGGW.

Purdy, L. (2006). Women's reproductive autonomy: Medicalisation and beyond. *Journal of Medical Ethics*, *32*(5), 287–291. https://doi.org/10.1136/jme.2004.013193

Reuters. (2016, April 12). Council of Europe raps Italy over difficulty in obtaining abortions. *Reuters*. https://uk.reuters.com/article/us-italy-abortion-idUKKCN0X820O

Sejm. (2017a). *Obywatelski projektustawy o zmianie ustawy z dnia 7 stycznia 1993 r. o planowaniu rodziny, ochronie płodu ludzkiego i warunkach dopuszczalności przerywania ciąży* [Citizens' draft bill amending the Act of 7 January 1993 on family planning, protection of the human fetus and conditions for the termination of pregnancy]. Druk nr 2146. http://sejm.gov.pl/Sejm8.nsf/page.xsp/archiwum

Sejm. (2017b). *Obywatelski projektustawy o prawach kobiet i świadomym rodzicielstwie* [Civic bill on women's rights and conscious parenthood]. Druk nr 2060. http://sejm.gov.pl/Sejm8.nsf/page.xsp/archiwum

Sejm. (2018). *Interpelacja nr 8508 – tekst odpowiedzi* [Interpelation No. 8508 – text of the answer]. Druk nr 2060. http://sejm.gov.pl/Sejm8.nsf/page.xsp/archiwum

Sheldon, S. (2016). The decriminalisation of abortion: An argument for modernisation. *Oxford Journal of Legal Studies*, *36*(2), 334–365. https://doi.org/10.1093/ojls/gqv026

Siegel, R. (1992). Reasoning from the body: A historical perspective on abortion regulation and questions of equal protection. *Stanford Law Review*, *44*(2), 261–381. https://doi.org/10.2307/1228947

Singh, S., Remez, L., Sedgh, G., Kwok, L., & Onda, T. (2018). *Abortion Worldwide 2017: Uneven Progress and Unequal Access*. Guttmacher Institute. https://www.guttmacher.org/sites/default/files/report_pdf/abortion-worldwide-2017.pdf

Supreme Court. (2018). *PRESS SUMMARY In the matter of an application by the Northern Ireland Human Rights Commission for Judicial Review*. Supreme Court of Northern Ireland. https://www.supremecourt.uk/cases/docs/uksc-2017-0131-press-summary.pdf

Święchowicz M. (2014). Aborcja po polsku [Abortion the Polish way]. *Newsweek Poland*.

Tamma, P. (2018, May 24). Even where abortion is legal, access is not granted. European Data Journalism Network. https://www.europeandatajournalism.eu/News/Data-news/Even-where-abortion-is-legal-access-is-not-granted

Thomson, J. (2016). Abortion and same-sex marriage: how are non-sectarian controversial issues discussed in Northern Irish politics? *Irish Political Studies*, *31*(4), 483–501. https://doi.org/10.1080/07907184.2015.1103226

Torrisi, C. (2017). Abortion in Italy: how widespread 'conscientious objection' threatens women's health and rights. *Open Democracy 50.50 blogs*. https://www.opendemocracy.net/en/5050/abortion-italy-conscientious-objection/

Trybunal Konstytucyjny. (2017). *Sprawa K 13/17* [Constitutional Tribunal case K 13/17]. Trybunal Konstytucyjny. http://trybunal.gov.pl

TVN24. (2014). *Aborcja Na Wyciągnięcie Ręki* [Abortion At Your Fingertips]. TVN. https://www.tvn24.pl/…/aborcja-na-wyciagniecie-reki-w-internecie

Wojciechowski, P. (2016). Podziemie aborcyjne w Polsce kwitnie. Ciąże usuwają też anestezjolodzy [Abortion underground in Poland is blossoming. Terminations are performed even by anesthesiologists]. *Gazeta Wyborcza*. https://wyborcza.pl/7,87648,20314186,zasadzka-na-anestezjologa.html?disableRedirects=true

World Health Organization. (2017). *Global abortion policies database*. WHO.

World Health Organization. (2018). *Country profile: Malta, Global Abortion Policies Database*. WHO. https://abortion-policies.srhr.org/country/malta/

Żuk, P., & Żuk, P. (2017). Women's health as an ideological and political issue: Restricting the right to abortion, access to in vitro fertilization procedures, and prenatal testing in Poland. *Health Care for Women International*, *38*(7), 689–704. https://doi.org/10.1080/07399332.2017.1322595

Conceiving Contemporary Parenthood

With the global expansion of reproductive technologies, there are ever more ways to create a family, and more family types than ever before. This book explores the experiences of those persons – whether single, in a couple, or part of collective co-parenting arrangements; whether hetero- or homosexual; whether cis- or transgender – who are creating what has been termed 'new family forms' with reproductive 'assistance'.

Drawing on qualitative research from around the world, the book is particularly anchored in two bodies of social science scholarship – sociological and anthropological inquiries into the cultural impact of reproductive technologies on the one hand, and parenting culture studies on the other. It seeks to create fertile conversations between these fields of scholarship, highlighting the intersections in the ways we think about conceiving and caring for children in today's 'reproductive landscape'.

Focusing specifically on persons whose reproductive journeys do not conform to dominant scripts, the book traces the many ways in which intentions, expectations and technological developments contribute to changing and enduring conceptions of *good parenthood* in the twenty-first century. Taking a holistic perspective, the book presents deep insights into the experiences not only of (intending) parents, but also of donors, surrogates, medical professionals and activists. The collection will be of interest to an international readership of scholars of gender, reproduction, parenting and family life.

The chapters in this book were originally published as a special issue of *Anthropology & Medicine.*

Zeynep B. Gürtin is Lecturer at the Institute for Women's Health at University College London (UCL), UK. She is a sociologist of reproduction and gender and her work brings together changing social trends in fertility with women's own personal accounts of their expectations and experiences, to provide insights about contemporary reproduction and relationships. Her recent research has focused on single women's fertility options, including egg freezing and solo motherhood; motherhood after 40; and reproductive anxiety and choices.

Charlotte Faircloth is Associate Professor in the Social Research Institute at University College London (UCL), UK. From sociological and anthropological perspectives, her work has focused on parenting, gender and reproduction using qualitative and cross-cultural methodologies. This research has explored infant feeding, couple relationships, intergenerational relations and, recently, the impact of coronavirus on family life.